THE WEEKEND
CARPENTER

THE WEEKEND CARPENTER

PHILLIP GARDNER

NEW HOLLAND

First published in 1999 by
New Holland Publishers (UK) Ltd
London • Cape Town
Sydney • Auckland

24 Nutford Place
London W1H 6DQ
United Kingdom

80 McKenzie Street
Cape Town 8001
South Africa

Level 1, Unit 4,
14 Aquatic Drive
Frenchs Forest
NSW 2086
Australia

Unit 1A, 218 Lake Road
Northcote
Auckland
New Zealand

10 9 8 7 6 5 4 3 2

Editor: Ian Kearey
Editorial Assistant: Kate Latham
Designer and illustrator: Paul Griffin
Photographer: Edward Allwright

Managing Editor: Coral Walker

Reproduction by
PICA Colour Separation, Singapore

Printed and bound in Malaysia
by Times Offset (M) Sdn. Bhd.

*For Christopher Robinson of Leicester Square, London. A man
who many years ago taught me to use my eyes to observe both
shapes and details with a considered eye. I don't think he
undertook my visual education as a task or some sort of mission;
the knowledge was imparted more by way of osmosis. Also because,
like his near namesake from A.A. Milne's* Winnie-the-Pooh, *he has
always been willing to help his friends.*

ACKNOWLEDGEMENTS

The logistics in pulling a book of this nature together were
prodigious. Without the help from the members of the production
team at New Holland and the generosity of my many sponsors, I
would have produced a meagre pamphlet at best. So, many thanks
to the following:

Coral, for her tact, diplomacy, her ideas and consistent
encouragement.

Kate, for her cool efficiency in arranging everything.

Ed, the most professional photographer I've ever had the
pleasure of working with, never complaining when the day's
shoot went on late into the night and always getting the
lighting just perfect.

Paul, who, on top of attending every photo-shoot and
meeting, managed to turn my notional scribbles into clear
drawings that communicate the ideas behind them.

Ian, who knows far more about wood and carpentry
than I do, and even more about elegant prose.

And finally Chrisie, for his workshop expertise and the
splendid lunches. A fine team indeed.

And now, thank you to my carefully selected sponsors:

Power tools
Simon Kinder and Janet Croffey at **DEWALT**®
for supplying all the power tools used throughout
the book, not to mention the expert advice given
at all times.

Router table and all routing accessories
Steven Phillips, the Managing Director of
Trend Machinery and Cutting Tools Ltd, for
supplying the router table and a selection of
his excellent cutters.

Two-part epoxy glues and varnish
Tony Calvert and Martin Armstrong at SP Systems
for the epoxy glue and coatings, gloves and
mixing pots, expert tips from Martin and a wealth
of technical data.

Chisels, vice, cramps and marking tools
The entire team at Record Tools.

**General hand tools, including screwdrivers and
planes and, of course, a Stanley knife!**
Liz Blades (a wonderful name for a lady who sells knives)
from Stanley Tools.

Grinding jigs
Michael O'Donnell for supplying the amazingly accurate
grinding jig and wheel used for all tool grinding.

Ezylap diamond sharpening stone
Bill Tilbrook of Tilgear – never again will I use anything else!

Health and safety equipment
Doctor Harley Farmer of Tecmark Ltd for the respirator
and his general advice about healthy workshop
practice.

Workmates (the benches *not* the operatives)
Jeremy Linley and Jane Adler at Black and Decker.

Contents

INTRODUCTION 6
TOOLS AND EQUIPMENT 8
MATERIALS 14
BASIC TECHNIQUES 18

PROJECTS

Child's bed 28
Chair and footstool 34
Shelving unit 42
Bathroom accessories 48
Console table 54
Birdhouse 60
Single wardrobe 64
Screen 70
Waney shelves 76

Kitchen accessories 80
Stacking storage units 86
Corner cabinet 90
Picture rail shelf 96
Coffee table 100
Computer workstation 104
CD rack 110
Letter box 114
Vanity unit 118
Tall storage chest 124
Kitchen unit makeover 130
Wall cupboard 136

TEMPLATES 141
SUPPLIERS 142
CONVERSION TABLE 143
INDEX 143

Introduction

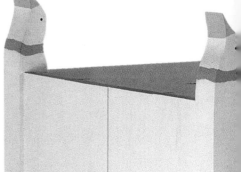

This book is intended for both the novice 'weekend carpenter' and those who have some basic skills and want to improve the scope and quality of their work. Hopefully, the newcomer will discover an insight into how to design and construct individual pieces of furniture for the home and garden – everything I suggest as a project is both cost-effective and reasonably simple to achieve, using an absolute minimum of complicated joints or techniques – while more experienced readers will pick up ideas about contemporary design, which they can then adapt to more advanced working methods, should they wish.

While all the projects can be constructed exactly as the designs shown using the suggested methods and techniques, not all the items will be to everybody's requirements, and adaptations from the basics are always possible. If you have a home computer with a relevant drawing package, the battle is half won, as simple rectangles and arcs can be drawn in moments. Otherwise, scale drawings or card models can help to modify the designs; the easiest scale to work to being 1:10. Note that the measuring conventions used throughout the book are always length first, followed by width, and then thickness.

On a practical note, I would like to emphasise that in all the photographs of power tools, any safety guards have been removed for the sake of clarity. At all times I would stress and stress again the importance of following any recommendations provided by tool manufacturers or hire shops regarding health and safety – garnished with some common sense, of course. Remember, I'm not going to be in your workshop to shout, 'Don't do that!'

On the following pages, you will find general information about materials and the tools you'll need, as well as basic techniques – these will be invaluable to the newcomer, and a useful reference to the more experienced hobbyist. There follows more than 25 projects to make, from simple kitchenware to an ambitious chest of drawers.

For anyone who enjoys carpentry as a hobby, this book will – I hope – come as a breath of fresh air, with pages and pages of contemporary and stylish furniture that you will love to have in your home, and that can be made in one weekend, or across several.

Tools and equipment

Any hobby is going to entail the purchase of some equipment. The basic toolkit — a set of screwdrivers, hammer, electric drill, etc., — does not need to be explained in detail; what I want to discuss here are the more specialized tools needed to complete some of the projects in this book.

Don't fall into the common trap of finding tools so attractive that you buy ones for which you have no real need. Instead, build up a kit slowly, always buying the best quality and brand that you can afford.

Where to buy your tools also needs consideration. Market stalls and car boot or garage sales are good hunting grounds for bargain-priced secondhand tools, but rarely for new tools, as these tend to be poor-quality imports or copies. You need to have a reasonable knowledge of tools before buying in such places, as there are no guarantees and faults may not be immediately apparent.

Large DIY stores have a wide range of reasonably priced tools, but for specialized, quality equipment you will have to visit a dedicated tool merchant, usually staffed — in my experience — by helpful, knowledgeable staff. Many of the larger stores have an excellent mail-order service. Buy tools from well-known manufacturers with a reputation for quality, as they will want to maintain it.

HAND TOOLS

These are rarely employed in professional workshops, as the demands of productivity preclude their use. But for the cost-conscious weekend carpenter they are a sensible starting point.

Marking and measuring tools should always be of the best quality. You will need a steel tape and rule, sliding bevel, knife, marking gauge and square. Always check the accuracy of a square; I have seen cheap versions of my 100 mm square with a blade inaccuracy of 1 mm over the short length of the blade. If you use a tool such as this, your work will never be true, and you will waste your time and materials. Further options would be a mortise gauge and some

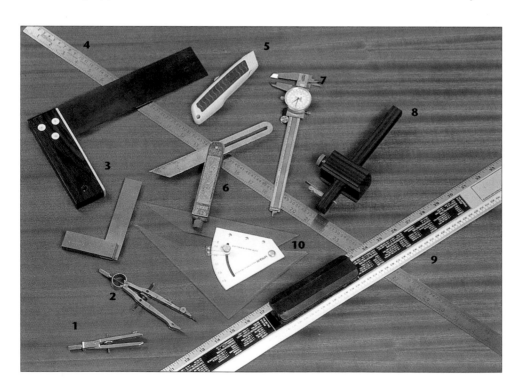

Marking & measuring:
1 dividers, 2 pair of compasses, 3 squares, 4 steel rule, 5 knife, 6 sliding bevel, 7 vernier gauge, 8 marking gauge, 9 straightedge, 10 adjustable set square

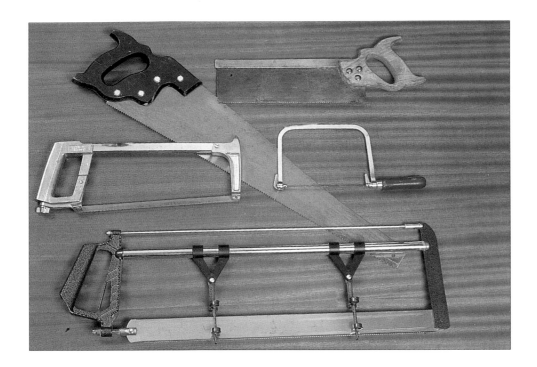

basic drafting tools, such as an adjustable set square and a pair of compasses and dividers.

A good basic kit of **saws** would consist of a crosscut or general-purpose saw (I don't recommend the disposable 'hard point' type, as these saws are mainly for site work and cannot be sharpened), tenon saw (the better models of these have a brass back), coping saw, and a hacksaw for cutting metal. Good additions to your kit would be a frame mitre saw and, for fine work, a dovetail saw (a smaller version of a tenon saw). Buy a mitre saw that can cut compound mitres, as the additional expense is well worth it: one will pay for itself in terms of time saved (for example, see the Vanity Unit on page 118).

Chisels can be bought in sets and are of two basic types, bevel-edge and firmer. The bevel-edge chisel is a light tool that gives increased control and accuracy; the side bevels allow one to cut into tight corners.

Firmers are the chisels you hit; the blade is far stronger and can be used in a robust manner. If you buy the 'split-proof' variety, they can take repeated mallet or hammer blows with no damage.

Other additions to the toolkit include a gouge (a chisel with a curved section), a mortise chisel (for removing the waste from a deep mortise), a wide range

of screwdrivers and a bradawl.

Planes are, perhaps, the most difficult hand tools for the novice to master. A common misconception about planes is that you can buy one, sharpen it and then achieve the silky-smooth finish of the cabinet-maker in moments. You can't. The plane is a precision tool made of finely calculated components, but to achieve the accuracy and ease of use you require, it will need even further refining. When a plane is made, the casting will be machined flat, but it is never truly flat. The blade also will have imperfections

Planes & scrapers: *1 jack plane, 2 flat cabinet scraper, 3 shoulder plane, 4 smoothing plane, 5 gooseneck cabinet scraper, 6 spokeshave, 7 block plane*

Chisels & screwdrivers:
1 firmer chisels, 2 bevel-edge chisels, 3 slot-head screwdrivers, 4 bradawl, 5 cross-head screwdrivers, 6 gouge, 7 mortise chisel, 8 Yankee screwdriver

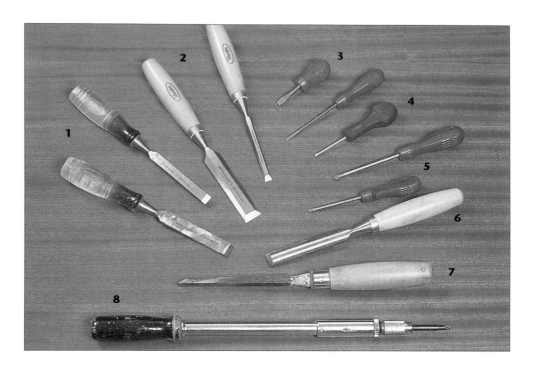

and will need polishing. These faults should be corrected and adjusted before any plane is used.

There are several basic types of plane. The jack plane, available in two widths, is used for achieving a flat, level surface quickly. The smoother, or smoothing plane, is a shorter version of a jack plane; buy one of these when you start working in hardwoods. The block plane is a small and incredibly useful item; the angle of the blade is shallower than other planes, and this tool is essential for planing end grain.

The shoulder plane is good for cleaning up the shoulders of tenons. A spokeshave — used for shaping surfaces — is a tricky tool to use, and is unnecessary if you are planning to buy an electric belt sander.

Two cabinet scrapers are shown in the photograph on page 9 — flat and gooseneck. These are superb woodworking tools, essential for hardwoods, but they are quite difficult for the novice to sharpen, until suddenly one day, almost as if by magic, you get the hang of it.

Drill bits: *these can often be bought in sets. The red case holds HSS bits, the grey case contains 'spur' or wood bits. The remaining pieces include 1, 5 multi-speed bits, 2 hole cutter, 3 flat bits, 4 countersink bit, 6 plug cutters.*

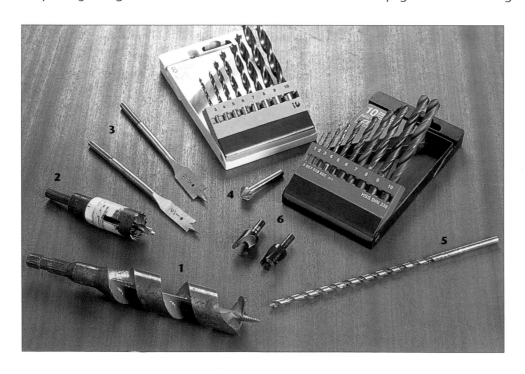

Of course, all these tools will need to be sharpened and maintained. This is covered on page 24. You will need at least one good-quality **sharpening stone**, preferably an industrial diamond type.

A range of G-cramps and sash **cramps** will also be required, as well as a carpenter's vice or a workbench of some description. A Workmate or portable workbench is a good compromise for the latter, at least in the early days.

POWER TOOLS

Virtually every carpenter will own at least one electric drill. These can be either powered straight from the mains or on a battery. The latter is more expensive, but much easier to use as you are not restricted to trailing lengths of cable. The minimum power required is 12 volts with a quick (one-hour) charge.

For each job, you will need a selection of **drill bits**. These are designed for masonry, metal or wood and graduate in 1 mm increments. High-speed-steel bits, normally called HSS bits are general-purpose bits, used for both wood and metal. 'Spur' or wood bits have a flatter cutting profile with a small point or spur in the centre. This locates the centre of the drill, stopping the bit from 'wandering'.

Flat bits offer a crude but effective method for the drilling of larger-diameter holes when accuracy is not imperative.

A hole cutter is pricey, but accurate and long-lasting; it will cut both wood and metal.

The multi-speed bit is also quite expensive and is only really necessary if you envisage doing a lot of work with the same size drill, such as fitting cylinder locks.

Also of use are plug cutters, employed in the making of the Chair and Footstool on page 34 and the Duckboard on page 53. A slightly better type with four cutters is also available, with the advantage of being self-centring.

A **jigsaw** is an essential tool. Buy one that has an electronic variable speed, giving greater control for curved cutting, and an adjustable pendulum cut — useful for ripping down the grain or coarse cutting of plywood. Another feature to look for is a method of clearing sawdust from the cut line, usually by blowing the dust away. Blades can be bought in mixed packs, but I tend to buy just the types I need for a particular job, fine-toothed scrolling blades being a favourite. Carbon-steel blades are the best by far. The black plastic plate is a shield that fits over the metal shoe of the saw, preventing any scratching on timber. The

The fine teeth of scrolling blades enable the **jigsaw** *to be used for cutting elaborate curves. This model is fitted with a dust extractor adapter.*

Blades for a **circular saw** *(left) are available in diameters from about 150–256 mm. An* **electric plane** *is useful, but not essential for the newcomer.*

*This **router** is a medium-size model with a fully adjustable fence. Also shown is a small range of cutters and guide bushes (to be used in conjunction with plywood or MDF templates).*

small clear plastic part is a anti-split device: because the jigsaw cuts on the up stroke, it can tear delicate timbers or plywood when cutting across the grain; this plate, inserted around the blade, minimises that effect.

A **circular saw** and **electric plane** are good additions to the kit, but they are not an immediate necessity. A range of blades is available for the circular saw: crosscut, ripping or combination. There is also a fine-finish blade, giving a quality of cut that just needs the barest planing subsequently. Always buy blades with tungsten tips.

Sanding machines will make the tedious aspects of carpentry more bearable. There are three basic types: the belt sander, the palm or orbital sander, and a small triangular tool called a detail sander. The belt sander illustrated on the opposite page is fitted with a sanding frame, which allows regular removal of waste on a flat surface without 'dishing'. It is an excellent attachment, but it doesn't replace a plane! Orbital sanders come in a range of sizes and finishing capabilities; essentially, the smaller the circular motion of the sanding plate, the finer the finish. A detail sander (not shown here) is useful for awkward access work.

The **router** has – in recent years – been wholeheartedly embraced by the home carpenter. It is a sort of cross between a drill and a jigsaw, but on the other hand, like neither. It is actually a hand-held version of a machine from the joiner's shop called a spindle moulder, with a chuck, like a drill, called a collet. Cutters are placed in the collet like a drill bit, the main difference being that once the cutter has entered the surface of the timber, you can move the tool and cutter in any direction. This enables you to cut channels through the middle of the timber or intricate mouldings

*Like routers, there are many designs of **router table** on the market. The main requirements are that the table and fence should be strong and sturdy.*

*The strong edge-to-edge joints that can be achieved by using a **biscuit jointer** make the tool ideal for joining boards to make table tops.*

on the edges with superb accuracy. Even though these tools have only recently started to have a huge impact on the home market, they have been in existence since the early 1900s. Consequently, the range of accessories and cutters is vast, with constant additions to both. This enables the home carpenter to have access to the sophisticated machining possibilities of the joiner's shop, giving a great saving in time and money.

Once equipped with a router and some good quality cutters, you might wish to invest in a **router table**. The router is mounted under the table with the cutter protruding above the table, allowing the timber to be manually pushed past the cutter. Look for one of sturdy construction with a comprehensive instruction manual.

Another time-saving device is a **biscuit jointer**. This is a small circular saw with a thicker than normal blade that cuts a groove to a predetermined depth. Small oval 'biscuits' are then glued in the groove, bridging two adjoining pieces of timber and providing a strong joint, either edge-to-edge, at right angles or at any division of a right angle.

An electric **grinding wheel**, while not an essential item, will prove a boon when putting a hollow-ground edge on planes and chisels. Combined with a quality grinding jig, it will take any guesswork out of achieving razor-sharp tools.

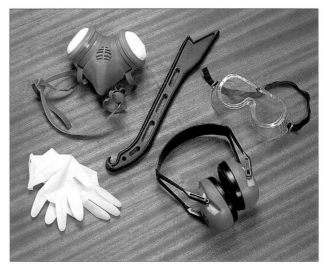

A basic health and safety kit (clockwise from bottom left): surgical gloves, respirator, push stick (for pushing wood through a circular saw or table-mounted router), goggles and ear protectors.

Most power tools can be hired by the week or the weekend. In my experience, it is usually better to hire from a small independent company as the big chains more frequently service large construction companies that tend to hire for long periods, and short-term hire often works out more expensive. Sometimes the tools are voltage-rated for use on construction sites as well, which may mean you have to hire a transformer.

An **orbital sander** (left) and a **belt sander** (right). Sanding sheets for both types appear below.

WORKING SAFELY

Health and safety is a vital consideration when using power tools. It's no good gaining time if you then shorten your life (or arm) by not taking the correct precautions to protect yourself. For example, the dust produced when machining timber or man-made boards can be harmful if inhaled. Therefore, a proper respirator mask that encloses both mouth and nose is essential.

Materials

TIMBER AND BOARDS

Essentially there are two types of timber: softwood and hardwood. Hardwood is by far the more expensive, but for some furniture it is the only realistic material. Softwood embraces the various species of pine and is sold in a vast array of stock sizes and qualities. It is sold as either 'sawn' – unfinished and rough — or PAR (planed, or prepared, all round). The size quoted is always of the sawn section. When the timber has been planed on all four faces to achieve the PAR state, the section has been reduced by about 5 mm in both directions; 50 x 50 mm PAR is, in fact, about 45 x 45 mm. Only buy sawn timber if you want to feature the rough finish, as with the Corner Cabinet on page 90.

For simple tasks, such as the Child's Bed on page 28, you can buy PAR timber from an ordinary builders' merchant or a DIY store. However, always remember that the stock size will have lost that few millimetres!

In the main, buy your timber from a good local builders' merchants or timber yard. These should have a policy of allowing you to select your own timber, and you'll soon develop a good relationship with the sales staff. If you tell them what you need the wood for (furniture), they will help you select the best lengths and quality. Look for defects such as splits, cupping (warping across the width), winding, large knots and small black dead knots, and politely reject any timber of this sort.

The sources above are also the places to buy beading, mouldings, dowels and boards or sheet material. Many places will cut boards to size, although they may insist that you buy the entire sheet when cut.

Prior to starting work, timber should be left in the workshop or home for a week or so, to acclimatize to the ambient temperature. Always stack your wood flat and support it well.

For hardwoods and paper-backed or iron-on veneers, you will need to visit a more specialized merchant; these are usually advertised in the Yellow Pages or woodworking magazines. A visit to your local joinery works or cabinetmaker will prove useful, as they often sell on small quantities of excess timber at reasonable rates. The same criteria regarding defects and storage apply as to softwoods.

Hardwoods: *1 burr maple, 2 ash, 3 walnut, 4 American oak, 5 maple, 6 mahogany*

Hardwood and softwood mouldings and pine, shown here in both sawn and PAR states

board with a surface that will rarely require more than a light sanding in preparation.

You can, of course, use reclaimed materials. Purchase them from a respectable merchant, or better still, keep your eyes open for building sites where places are being renovated — restaurant and bar refurbishments tend to be the most rewarding hunting grounds. Just ask the site foreman what is being sold off: hardwood doors, counters and strip flooring are firm favourites. You will have to arrange transport and storage and then undertake the onerous task of de-nailing, which is extremely tedious, but you'll save a fortune.

Of the boards used in this book, MDF (medium-density fibreboard) is a smooth, highly stable board that finishes very well. Always check that the corners haven't been damaged or that steel packing bands have not destroyed the edges, and reject any board that is offered with these defects. Shuttering ply is probably the cheapest form of board available, used in the construction industry for boarding up and making moulds for pouring concrete. Only use this board when the surface will be completely covered, as featured in the Kitchen Unit Makeover on page 130.

Birch-faced plywood is a reasonably priced

(From the top): Paper-backed veneer, birch-faced ply, MDF and shuttering ply are the sheet materials used in this book.

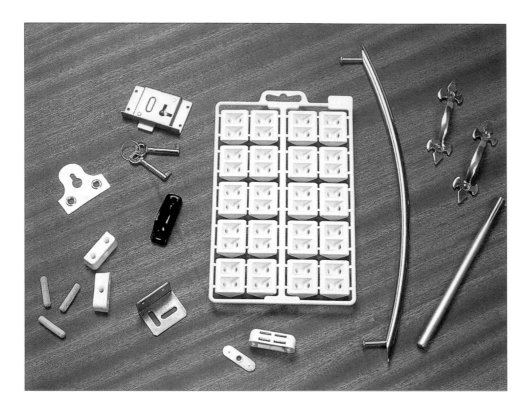

Ironmongery: *Corner blocks, dowels, stretcher plates, mirror plates, magnetic catches and other such fixings can be purchased inexpensively at DIY stores.*

These will supply most fittings, such as hinges in good-quality brass or stainless steel. The stainless steel rod used in the Waney Shelves on page 76 can be bought from a non-ferrous stockholder and cut to length with a hacksaw. Stockholders can be found in the Yellow Pages.

IRONMONGERY

As a catch-all heading, ironmongery is a bit of a misnomer, as many fittings are often made of plastic or brass. However, this category does include all the traditional items associated with fixing timber, ie, screws, nails and nuts and bolts.

The large DIY stores tend to have the widest range of fixings and fittings, and most stock the products you will require for simple furniture making: magnetic catches, mirror plates, small dowels and door furniture. Just about everything is sold in small packs, and you might have to buy in multiples when you only need one or two items. These packs can also work out quite expensive when compared to buying one or two of the same piece from a specialist ironmonger.

There are some items that you will only find in a specialist store. Usually, however, these stores are not open at weekends and the waiting time during the week can be lengthy; a 45-minute queue to buy a hinge is not uncommon in my local suppliers. A good solution is to enquire if they provide a mail-order service – most do.

A good source for many items is a boat chandler's.

I usually buy a box of 100 or 200 screws for a job and put the surplus in a large plastic, compartmentalized box. This means always having some to hand.

Don't be tempted to make do with fittings and fixings that obviously weren't designed for the purpose – match the materials to the job.

16

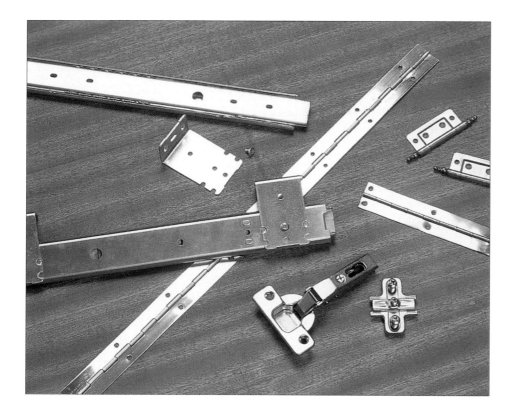

The more specialized fittings, such as keyboard tray sliders, drawer runners and flush hinges can be purchased by mail order.

conjunction with timber as a combination filler and adhesive. Buy it from a car paint supplier, where it should be considerably cheaper than a DIY store.

Filler adhesive needs to be applied with a mastic gun and is sold under a variety of brand names. It is expensive, and once the tube is opened it goes off quite quickly, but it is ideal for rapidly fixing timber that is not under any great stress.

ADHESIVES

The vast array of wood adhesives on the market can be simplified for the weekend carpenter. First, my favourite — two-part epoxy — a remarkably strong glue. It is mainly used in boatbuilding and is widely available from chandlers' or surf shops. Unfortunately, it is quite expensive.

You need to measure out the two components precisely and be aware of the ambient temperature. Use either plastic syringes or clear plastic containers marked on the side with graduations. Clear plastic 35 mm film canisters make ideal mixing pots for small amounts. The wearing of surgical gloves is advisable when mixing and applying epoxy, simply to protect your hands as the glue is difficult to remove from skin. When you use epoxy for the first few times, refer to the free data sheets provided.

PVA (polyvinyl acetate), the everyday white liquid glue available in plastic tubes and tins, can also be purchased in a water-resistant version. Easy to use and cheap, it is not terribly strong, but adequate for most interior work.

Two-part filler, the elastic type, is often used in

Cascamite, a white, powdered resin glue mixed with water, is waterproof, dries clear, and is cheap and easy to use. Wear gloves when applying. It may have a different brand name locally.

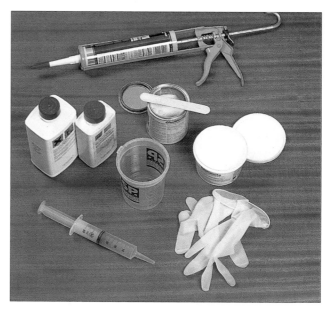

Modern glues *for woodworking: follow the manufacturer's directions for use at all times.*

Basic techniques

I have kept this section simple, passing on some short-cuts and tips I've learnt over the years, knowing that as you start working with wood, you will learn from the inevitable mistakes far better than any amount of book learning. There isn't a carpenter, or even for that matter a cabinetmaker, in the land who hasn't learnt by the same process.

MARKING OUT

When your timber is ready to work, you need to sort it into the best lengths for the job, taking into account the position of any knots; you don't want a knot where, at a later date, you will want to cut a mortise or other joint. Also, study the grain pattern, especially in hardwoods, and select it to the best advantage for the design.

The best tip ever: **'Measure twice, cut once.'** Keep checking a measurement until you are absolutely sure before cutting.

Mark the proscribed length, leaving a small excess at each end, then square round from the marks using a pencil and a square. If the marks don't line up perfectly, this means the wood is warped or in wind (where the timber has started to spiral along its length) and this

will have to be rectified. Choose the best face and edge and then mark accordingly.

A marking gauge is used to cut or score a line parallel to the edge of a piece of timber. Hold the stock firmly against the edge of the timber and roll the spur into the wood. Be aware of the direction of the grain and run the tool along the timber in such a way that the grain pulls the point of the gauge away from the stock.

A mortise gauge is a similar tool; here, two parallel lines are scored simultaneously, defining the waste portions of a tenon and the mortise. By using the same setting to mark both parts of the joint, in theory a perfect fit is always obtained.

To mark an oblique line, use a sliding bevel, which has an adjustable blade that allows you to set and repeat any angle at will.

A rod is a simple measuring stick and is described in more detail above right. This is used when making up mortise-and-tenoned frames, as in the Wall Cupboard on page 136.

When marking shelves or anything that has a left and right pair, ensure that you mark each piece as such. It helps to lay out the components on the bench or

Mortise gauge: *a marking device with twin spurs*

Marking gauge: *used to mark a thickness*

USING A MEASURING ROD

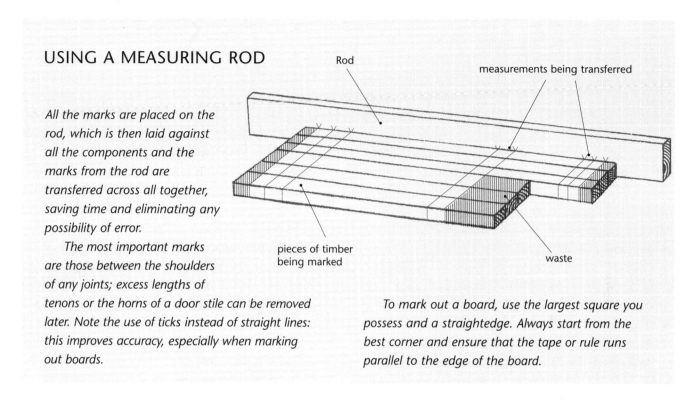

Rod
measurements being transferred
pieces of timber being marked
waste

All the marks are placed on the rod, which is then laid against all the components and the marks from the rod are transferred across all together, saving time and eliminating any possibility of error.

The most important marks are those between the shoulders of any joints; excess lengths of tenons or the horns of a door stile can be removed later. Note the use of ticks instead of straight lines: this improves accuracy, especially when marking out boards.

To mark out a board, use the largest square you possess and a straightedge. Always start from the best corner and ensure that the tape or rule runs parallel to the edge of the board.

floor and visualise how they fit together prior to marking out housings and rebates, etc.

For the sake of clarity, all marking out in this book has been done with a black felt pen. Normally a sharp HB or hard pencil will do, except where accuracy is essential. In these cases use a knife – a Stanley knife is fine – but a cabinetmaker will always use a dedicated marking knife. This has a cutting edge on one side only, allowing the knife to rest precisely against the steel rule or square.

PREPARING TIMBER BY HAND

As long as you have selected it carefully, planed softwood will require minimum preparation – usually just light planing to remove small ridges that run across the grain as a result of the timber being machined too quickly.

If you buy hardwoods ready-machined, the same will apply, but this is expensive. Preparing hardwood yourself takes diligence and is not easy.

For perfect preparation of hardwoods, cut the timber slightly overlength and secure it level in a vice. Use a jack plane to get the best face perfectly flat. The

edge of the plane's sole can be used as a guide to assess low points, both across the grain and along it. Hold the plane tilted at 45 degrees on the timber and look for any gaps under the plane. If you can see light anywhere, this means that you have a low spot and the rest of the wood will need to be planed down to that lowest level.

To check for straightness over the length, lay two flat and parallel winding sticks across the timber at front and back; sight down the timber from one end, making sure that the tops of both sticks are parallel to each other. If not, the timber should be planed diagonally, taking off the high points.

Once you have achieved a flat surface, turn the timber in the vice so that the best edge is uppermost. Plane the edge true and square to the first face. Use the plane to check for light showing through, but also use a square to ensure that the edge remains at 90 degrees to the planed face. Release from the vice and mark with face and edge marks.

Hold the stock of a marking gauge hard against the finished face and slide the bar back and forth until the spur is the required distance from the face. At no point

Marking the face and edge

should the timber be thinner than this set distance. Lock the gauge and, holding the timber against the bench, slightly roll the gauge so that the spur leaves a cut line in the edge. Do this on all four edges.

Replace the timber in the vice and plane the other face down to the lines. When this face is flat and parallel to the other, set your marking gauge to the desired width, mark across both faces and ends with the stock tight against the face edge, and plane down to the marks once more. After you have done all this, you should have a flat, true and square piece of timber.

PLANING

When planing, keep the shavings fine by controlling the adjusting nut, and be aware of the direction of the grain – plane with the grain at all times. In most timbers you can see the grain direction by looking at the edges: if the grain on the edge runs up to the left-hand side of the face, you will have to plane from right to left, and the reverse is obviously true. This method is not infallible, as sometimes in the middle of a piece you will find what is known as 'wild grain'. In some timbers, such as mahogany, this can be seen as a slightly darker area, and a very light brush with your fingertips will confirm it. Wild grain can be combated in two ways: try planing with the plane at 45 degrees to the direction of travel, or rub a small amount of beeswax across the sole.

The block plane is held in the palm of one hand and used to plane end grain and to put an arris on timber. An arris is a small bevel used as a detail or, on painted furniture, to prevent the paint from being knocked off the corners.

For rapid and effortless planing use an electric plane; the same principles apply as for a hand plane, with the addition that you must be careful when starting and finishing a pass. If the body dips at all when coming to the edge of the timber, an ugly gouge will result.

Never use an electric plane closer than about 0.5 mm to the finished line, and always finish with a jack plane as you have greater control and a far superior finish.

All electric planes have a fine depth adjuster, but I tend to use my left-hand forefinger and thumb for superfine adjustment of the cut depth with a slight upward pressure. I also adjust the level of the sole with this hand when planing a bevel. Always keep your

Skew the plan at 45 degrees to combat wild grain

Using a block plane to create an arris

hands well away from the blades and check that the blade rest (if fitted) is in position before setting the tool down.

CABINET SCRAPING

As mentioned earlier, cabinet scraping is an essential technique to master when finishing hardwoods. Although at first glance a cabinet scraper looks just like a square of plain steel, all four edges have a very slight angle ground on them which leaves a burr. After burnishing the burr, a sharp cutting edge is achieved.

Hold the tool in both hands at about 45 degrees to the timber and slightly flex it. As you push (or pull) the tool along the work, very fine shavings will be removed. If you remove dust as opposed to shavings, your scraper needs sharpening (see page 24). Don't run the scraper absolutely in line with the grain, always at a slight angle, varying the direction with each stroke, but never scrape at right angles to the grain.

The finish left by a well-sharpened scraper is incomparable; the tool is also used to disguise tears in the surface of the timber. To do this you will have to gradually dish the surface to the depth of the tear.

The main problem with using a cabinet scraper is that it becomes warm with friction quickly, and you must take care not to burn your thumbs.

CHISELLING

Work that needs to be chiselled will usually be done in one of two ways. First, cutting – or more correctly, par-

Paring the cheeks of a tenon

ing – in a horizontal plane. A typical example for this would be smoothing the cheeks of a sawn tenon.

For this type of paring, the work must always be mounted in the vice or securely clamped to the bench. Keep the tool level and grip the cutting end tightly, exerting a downward pressure with your thumb. Start each thin slice with a corner of the cutting edge and slide the tool across any high points. The back of the chisel must always lie flat against the surface – if you lift the handle while cutting, you will dig into the timber.

The final cut will use the line made by the mortise gauge as a starting point, and the edge of the chisel will slot into the cut line at the front on the end grain. As you push forwards towards the shoulder of the tenon, be aware of the gauge lines at each side; as these come into view from the top, it is time to stop. Finally, by

Finishing hardwood with a cabinet scraper

Horizontal paring of the grain

pressing down hard with your thumb, assess any high points in the middle and remove them with a slicing action.

When removing waste from timber that can be approached from both sides, such as a housing or dovetail socket, chisel to just past the middle of the cut then approach it from the other side. Repeat this technique until you have cut down to the gauge lines. This will leave a small hump in the middle, which is removed at the end. To retain full control of the tool, take a small slice at a time.

The other technique is vertical paring; this is the same as horizontal paring, except that here the work is placed on the bench with the chisel held vertically and downward pressure removes the waste. Always protect the surface of the bench by using a small piece of card or waste timber. Generally speaking, vertical paring is used to remove waste in a speedy fashion, changing to horizontal paring when you approach the final line or when greater accuracy is required; however, personal preference will play a part as to which method finds favour with you.

SAWING

Always make sure that the work is well supported and level. When using a power saw, make sure that the lead is long enough to complete the cut and that it will not get snagged.

A handsaw is held with the forefinger extended along the handle to guide the direction of the blade in

Jigsawing with a guide

both planes. When starting a cut, use the thumb of the other hand as a guide, with the tip of your thumb just up to the line and the extreme tip resting against the saw blade. Hold the handle with a loose grip and make a few gentle strokes back and forth, using the lower half of the blade to start the cut. Western handsaws cut when they are pushed (Japanese models, however, cut when pulled), so let the saw do the work on the downstroke, using a smooth sweeping action, and pull the saw back effortlessly.

Always check that the blade's face remains at 90 degrees to the face of the work, and control this by use of your extended forefinger. When coming to the end of a cut, ensure that the offcut is held or supported in some way, so that it will not tear.

With all sawing, by hand or power, one of the most common mistakes is not paying attention to which side of a line you are cutting. Always mark the waste side and cut along the waste side of the line.

When cutting sheet material or ripping down a plank with an electric saw, use a guide clamped to the work. This is necessary for both circular saws and jigsaws, although with a circular saw ensure that the batten or clamps will not obstruct the passage of the saw's motor.

ROUTING

Whilst the router is often used as purely a means to machine decorative parts and edges, by far the most useful aspect for the weekend carpenter is its ability to cut precise joints every time, thereby overcoming a major skill barrier and allowing entry for all into the craft of woodworking. The array of cutters available will give you the capability to cut housings, rebates, mortise and tenons and dovetails – in fact, any of the simple joints used in this book.

Using a handsaw: note the extended forefinger which guides the direction of the blade

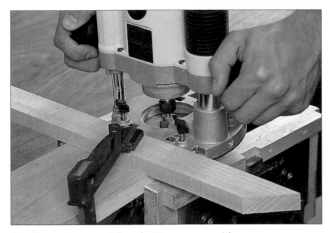

Routing a tenon with a batten as a guide

The direction of the feed is important

However, certain things must be kept in mind when using the tool; first, the cutter, fully exposed in most cases, rotates at a phenomenal speed. Take care and preferably use a plunge router, which allows the cutter to be withdrawn into the machine before and after each cut. Practise with the various cutters you buy on a piece of scrap wood before using them in earnest, partly to get used to the feel, but also to see just what each type of cutter can do. When making a cut, use two or three passes. If the wood smokes or the tone of the router drops, you are trying to remove too much material in one pass; stop, raise the cutter a little and try again. Always allow the router to achieve full speed before starting a cut, and never start a cut with the cutter up against the wood.

Most routers have a removable side fence; the

Using a template with a guide bush

addition of a further one is a great help when cutting mortises on the edge of timber, as it will stop the router rocking from side to side.

Some woodworkers can, after considerable practice, use a router freehand, much in the same way a jigsaw can be used, but the novice should always use a fence or guide of some sort. A batten clamped to the surface can suffice, but often the most common guide will be a template from a small piece of plywood or MDF, as in the CD Rack on page 110.

A template of this type will need to be used in conjunction with a guide bush; a selection of bushes is provided with better makes of router. Guide bushes are screwed to the underside of the router, with the cutter protruding through the bush. The outer edge of the guide bush is then held against the template, allowing repeated shapes to be cut with accuracy.

Another thing to understand is that the 'direction of feed' should always be against the direction in which the cutter rotates. The tip of the cutter should pull the timber along; if you rout in the other direction, there is a danger of the timber being pushed away from the cutter, resulting in an uneven cut and the potential of danger to yourself from the exposed cutter.

BISCUIT JOINTING

Biscuits are tightly compressed ovals made from beech which, when wetted with glue, expand into a slot pre-cut by the jointer and provide a strong method of joining timbers edge to edge. The biscuits come in three

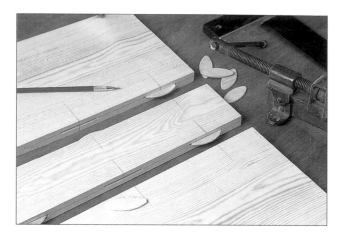

Using biscuits to join the parts of a table top

sizes, 0, 10 and 20, with size 0 being the smallest.

A benefit of the jointer is its built-in margin of error of about 6 mm. In addition, marking out is extremely simple, in most cases being just a small mark on the face of each timber to be joined.

You can use the biscuit jointer as a freehand tool with the work clamped down, or you can fix it to the bench with small blocks or screw through the sole plate (if holes are provided). In the latter case, the material to be slotted is then pushed up to the cutter.

SHARPENING TOOLS

There is not one project in this book that can be completed satisfactorily unless your tools are absolutely sharp.

For plane irons and chisels, a hollow-ground bevel

should be put on the edge first. The term 'hollow-ground' refers to the slightly dished profile that results from using a grinding wheel. It is possible to grind this primary bevel flat on a stone, but the ease with which you can put on a fine cutting edge later makes a huge difference to the finish and time taken. Set your jig to grind at 30 degrees and lay the plane iron or chisel against the jig as shown in the photograph below.

Slowly bring the tool into contact with the wheel, keeping it firmly pressed to the jig. When contact is made, slide the blade back and forth along the wheel, dipping the blade in water every couple of passes to keep it cool. This will avoid 'bluing' the steel; if the steel does blue, you must grind off all traces of the discoloration and start again – this is a waste of expensive tool steel, so take great care. After some time there is a possibility that your wheel will become pitted or grooved, in which case you will have to dress the wheel with a diamond dresser. Better-quality jigs will have an attachment that allow you to do this.

To put the honing edge on, use a honing guide on a diamond stone, as shown on page 25. Diamond stones may be an expensive option, but they do not dish like the more traditional stones, and consequently last far longer.

To achieve the sharper edge, the angle needs to be 25 degrees. Hold the chisel or plane iron as shown and move it back and forth, keeping the blade firmly pressed down on the stone.

When an even edge has been produced in this way,

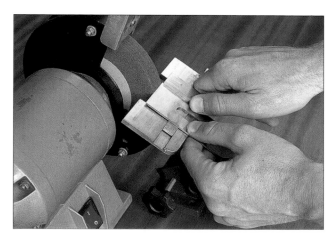

Sharpening a plane iron in a jig

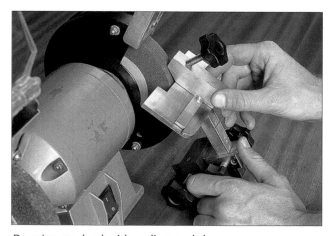

Dressing a wheel with a diamond dresser

Honing a chisel using a honing guide

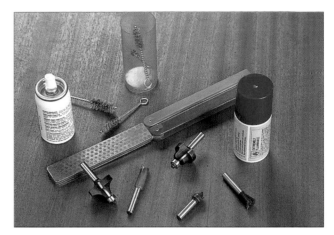

Cutters are kept sharp with a diamond stone and light oil

there will be a burr on the reverse of the tool, which must be removed by laying the back of the tool flat on the stone and rubbing back and forth. It is essential that the tool remains flat while doing this. When smooth, a fine burr is left on the extreme tip; this is removed by drawing the edge of the tool through some end grain, usually the end of a workbench.

As your skills improve, you will discover refinements of these basic techniques of sharpening.

All cabinet scrapers are manufactured sharp with the cutting burr ready to use; however, in use this will quickly dull and the tool will need to be resharpened. First, file the long edges square to the face, then put a bevel of about 80 degrees on using a stone; the photograph below left shows a carborundum stone for variety, but since I have acquired a diamond stone I have used that for all my tool sharpening.

At the very least, sharpen both long edges – some woodworkers do all four, it's up to you. This grinding creates the burr that provides the cutting edge, so do not remove it as one would with a plane or chisel. Next, rub the back of the burred edge with a bur-

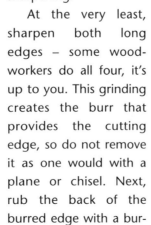

Sharpening a cabinet scraper

nisher. This burnisher is a rounded steel, similar to that used by a butcher in days of old to sharpen his knives with great dramatic effect. I always use the back of a gouge for this job, although there are some devices on the market that claim to make this job easier.

Router bits and electric saw blades can be sharpened using an ordinary diamond stone, but the small one featured in the photograph above right is particularly useful. Also pictured are some small wire brushes, PTFE spray and light oil. All these items can be kept together as a kit, with the express use of keeping your router cutters sharp and cutting at maximum efficiency.

SIMPLE JOINTS

All of the joints used in this book are simple enough for even the novice to accomplish quickly. I have used both housings and halving, mortise and tenon, machined dovetail and finger joints.

There are two fundamental points to remember when producing an accurately fitting joint. First, always mark from a designated face. This is why we mark face side and face edge – not only do they provide reference marks as to which is the most attractive face, but they also ensure that the two component parts of a joint will be measured equally from the front of the item being jointed. Second, remove waste carefully: to remove more is easy, to replace timber removed in error is not.

A **corner halving** is used to join two timbers of equal thickness together. The amount of waste removed from both parts is the same and you will

Simple joints. *Shown here are 'exploded' views of three basic joints used: in the foreground, a **corner halving**, used in the Corner Cabinet on page 90; on the right, a **stub mortise and tenon**, used in the Child's Bed on page 28; and at the top, a **haunched mortise and tenon**, used in the Wall Cupboard on page 136.*

create a shoulder on both parts, which will keep the two timbers at 90 degrees to each other. To determine the distance of the shoulders from the ends of both parts, proceed as follows:

Take one piece and lay it over the other, square to the lower piece at one end making an 'L' shape. Draw a line on the lower part where the upper one sits. Lay the two pieces side by side and copy the line across onto the other timber. Square both lines around all four sides of each part.

Divide the thickness of the timber in half and set a marking gauge to that dimension. Place the stock of the gauge against the face side and run a mark from the squared line on the edge up to the end grain, along the end grain and then down the other side. Repeat for the mating part. Crosshatch the waste: this will be the upper portion on one piece and the lower on the other.

Place the timber in the vice and saw down to the shoulder line with a tenon saw as shown below. Turn the timber around and cut from the other side. Then place the timber vertically and cut the hump that will be left in the centre, making sure that you do not cut below the line at the rear.

Place horizontally in the vice and saw the shoulder line down to the gauge mark, ensuring that you keep an eye on the line at the rear of the work. Then clean up the saw cuts using a chisel.

This joint can be positioned not only at a corner but also in any place along the length of timber, making a 'T' or an 'X' joint. In these cases the waste has to be removed with a chisel after making two parallel saw cuts at the shoulder marks.

To make a **mortise and tenon joint**, mark the

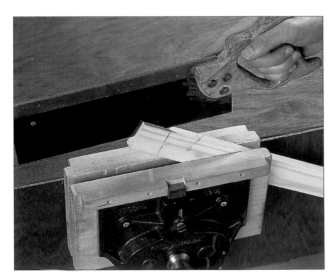

Sawing to the shoulder line of a halving joint

Sawing a tenon cheek

Top: through housing joint; bottom: stopped housing joint

shoulders of the tenon as above, but instead of dividing the thickness by two, divide by three. Saw the tenon cheeks as for the half lap, again finishing with a chisel.

For the mortise, use the gauge, again from the face side, to mark the full length of the mortise. Remove the waste down to the depth required, this being the same as the length of the tenon.

Use a drill bit with a diameter the same as the width of the mortise to remove the bulk of the waste. Then clean up the mortise hole with a chisel. For a far better finish, use a router. If you use a router the ends of the mortise will be rounded. Either square them off with a chisel or round off the corners of the tenon. (I usually do the latter, it's quicker and easier.)

If the tenon is a haunched or a **stub tenon**, place the timber vertically in the vice and saw down the grain at the relevant points. If you are not sure about how the two parts fit together, it helps to cut the tenon and then place it in position prior to marking out the mortise.

A **housing** is the term for a groove cut across the width of a timber. Normally, this would be to slot a shelf into as in the Shelving unit on page 42. The two types shown are a 'through housing' and a 'stopped housing', the purpose of a stopped housing being to give a neater front edge to your work.

Mark two parallel lines the full width of the timber into which you are going to cut a housing. These will be the shoulder lines and will be set apart the exact thickness of the shelf to be inserted.

Cut along the inside of the lines with a tenon saw down to the proscribed depth. (Usually halfway or a third into the thickness of the timber.) Use the straight cutting edge of the saw blade to assist getting the level cut all the way across the housing.

Remove the waste with a chisel, the first part with the cutting edge of the blade turned down. Approach from both ends working towards the middle, be careful not to cut into the shoulders in the early stages. A hump will be left in the middle of the channel; remove this by turning the chisel over and slicing the top until the entire channel is flat.

Hand-cutting a housing is arduous and time consuming, a router or circular saw with the blade set to the correct depth will complete this task in moments.

If using a circular saw for a stopped housing, the final part will still need to be cut by hand using a chisel and a mallet.

CUTTING MITRES

Mitres are 45-degree cuts in two parts which are then joined together with a biscuit or pins to form a right angle. The most basic method is to use a tenon saw in a mitre box, but this is rarely satisfactory because the saw can move from side to side – and when the box becomes worn with use, the error is compounded. A frame saw is a far better solution. Mark the cut with a combination square or a mitre square, and hold the timber firmly in the frame using a cramp. Take it slowly, and keep an eye on the line.

A compound mitre is a mitre with a bevel on two planes; this bevel is marked out and then planed with a sharp block plane.

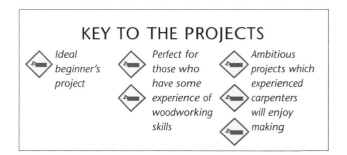

KEY TO THE PROJECTS

Ideal beginner's project

Perfect for those who have some experience of woodworking skills

Ambitious projects which experienced carpenters will enjoy making

Child's bed

This simple design uses low-cost materials, and a minimum skill level is required for the joints involved. The use of a router is recommended to cut the headboard housings. Although they can be cut by hand, it is a time-consuming business and a router will give you a far more professional finish.

The headboard and footboard could easily be adapted to your child's personal taste – for example, the headboard cut-out could be a silhouette of a favourite cartoon character; use a photocopier to enlarge a drawing and then paint the headboard to suit.

Before starting, take into account the size of mattress you will be using. I used one 2 m long by 800 mm wide, and all the measurements of the bed are designed to fit this size. If you use a different-size mattress, you will have to adapt the measurements.

I finished the bed by using a semi-matt paint on top of primer and undercoat, but you could use a colour wash or stain, or just varnish. Gloss paint, however, could soon look tatty.

Essential Tools

pencil, straightedge, tape, square, marking gauge, screwdriver, tenon saw, jigsaw, electric drill, 12 mm flat bit, 3 mm twist bit, 8 mm wood bit, 6 mm multi-speed bit (200 mm long), 12 and 25 mm bevel-edge chisels, mallet, block plane, Workmate or workbench, two sash cramps or two pairs of slow folding wedges

OTHER USEFUL TOOLS
mortise gauge, table-mounted circular saw, router with 12 mm straight cutter

Child's bed

The dimensions of this bed make it suitable for a child of up to about 14 or 15 years old. As with many of the other projects in this book, you can adapt the dimensions and lists of materials to suit your own requirements.

You'll need to know

MARKING OUT
p. 18

ROUTERS
p. 22

SAWING
p. 22

SIMPLE JOINTS
p. 25

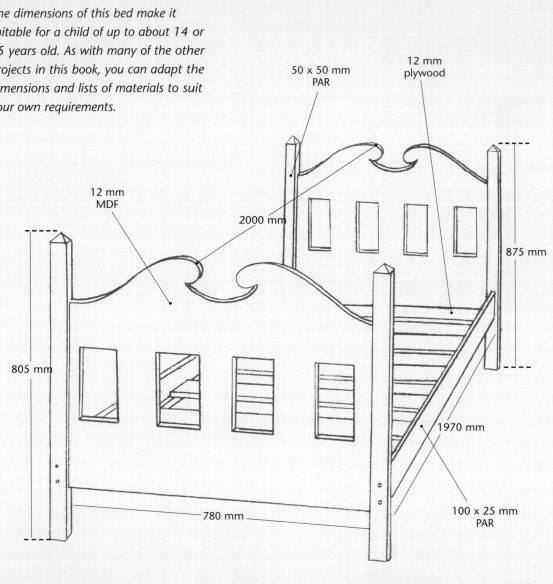

Materials

1220 x 810 x 12 mm MDF	2 pieces 2000 x 25 x 15 mm softwood lipping
10 pieces 800 x 100 x 12 mm plywood	16 countersink screws 25 mm x no 6
2 pieces 900 x 50 x 50 mm straight-grained pine or similar (PAR)	40 countersink screws 18 mm x no 6
2 pieces 850 x 50 x 50 mm straight-grained pine or similar (PAR)	8 'bunk-bed bolts' 100 mm
2 pieces 2100 x 100 x 25 mm straight-grained pine or similar (PAR)	PVA wood glue
	sandpaper grades 80 to 150

FIG 1

FIG 2

1 For the legs, you need two 900 mm and two 850 mm lengths of 50 x 50 mm timber. Lay all four lengths side by side, with the best face uppermost and one end of all four legs aligned. Mark these faces as your face sides. Lay a square as near to the end of the four legs as you can and draw a line across all of them. This is the base line of the legs, which will then need to be squared around each leg. Measure 205 mm from this line and draw another line across all four legs, to represent the bottom of the mortise for the side rails to enter. At this point you will need to measure accurately the true width of the 100 x 25 mm dimensioned timber, normally about 92 mm. Transfer this measurement to the legs so that the third line will be the width of the side rails along from the second line you drew. Transfer these two lines to the back of the legs. Set your mortise gauge to 12 mm between the pins, 15 mm from the stock to the nearest pin. Then mark as shown in Fig 1.

2 Separate the legs into two pairs and mark them left and right. On the inner face of each pair, mark out for the housings into which the headboard and footboard will fit. For the headboard mark a line 520 mm from the base line, and for the footboard a line 450 mm. Leave the pins of the mortise gauge set to 12 mm, but adjust the stock to 15 mm, and mark as shown in Fig 2.

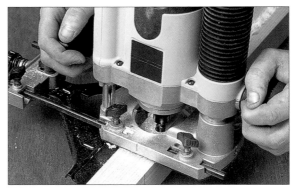

FIG 3

3 Clamp each leg to the bench, and use a router with a side fence to groove out the side channels to a depth of 15 mm (Fig 3). Turn each leg over and remove the mortise for the rails to a depth of 18 mm. Mark the full height of each leg – for the head pair this is 875 mm, and for the foot pair it is 805 mm. To finish the tops of the legs with a pyramid shape; measure 50 mm back from the top on each leg and make a 45-degree cut on all four sides. Cut the bottom of the legs to the line you first drew as the base line in step 1.

TIP

Bunk-bed bolts might be difficult to locate, so track them down before you begin. You should be able to obtain them from a good hardware supplier, who will be able to order them if they are not in stock. Look in your Yellow Pages or local telephone directory under 'Hardware Retailers'.

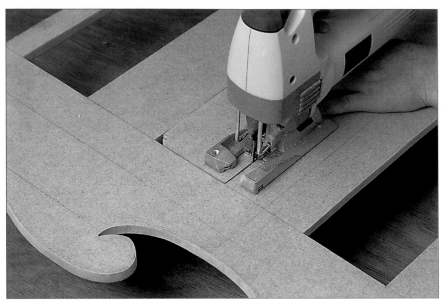

FIG 4

TIP

When drilling the holes for the bunk-bed bolts in the legs, you will find it easier and more efficient if you place the bed on the floor with one end pressed up against a wall.

4 From the 810 mm edge of the MDF sheet measure 580 mm square across and cut the board into two pieces; the smaller is the footboard. Working from the template on page 141, cut out the shape using a jigsaw fitted with a scrolling blade for the curves and a normal blade for the straight lines (see Fig 4). Repeat for the headboard, but remember to extend the template so that the overall height is 650 mm. Assemble each set of legs and board together and glue up, using sash cramps or slow folding wedges to hold the pieces in position.

5 Now take the two rails and cut them to a length of 2036 mm. Choose your face sides, turn them over and mark out for a stub tenon 18 mm long and 12 mm thick at each end. Use a tenon saw and a chisel to remove the waste, as shown in Fig 5. Next cut the two pieces of 25 x 15 mm softwood lipping to length and glue and screw them to the bottom of the rails using the 25 mm x no 6 gauge screws. Wipe away any excess glue before it has a chance to dry, and assemble the rails to the head and footboard assemblies.

FIG 5

FIG 6

FIG 7

6 The two lines transferred in step 1 enable you to line up the bolts with the tenons. Find the centre of the legs and drill two holes evenly spaced with the 6 mm bit. Drill through the leg, through the tenon and into the rail, keeping the drill square to the leg (Fig 6). Use tape as a depth gauge on the bit so that you only drill the length of the bolts. Repeat this process on the other three legs.

FIG 8

7 Once the bed is assembled you will now have to insert the cylindrical nuts for the bunk-bed bolts. This can be a little tricky to get right because, no matter how careful you have been to keep your drill square in step 6, some error will almost certainly have occurred. For ease of explanation, this step is shown in more detail (see Fig 7). Insert the bolts into the holes, leaving about 30 mm protruding. Use a square or a straightedge to sight the top and bottom of each bolt, then draw two sets of parallel lines and make a mark across them about 10 mm short of the length of the bolts. Drill an 8 mm hole through this mark to receive the cylindrical nut. Insert the nuts and screw up the bolts, but be careful not to overtighten them at this stage.

8 Cut the plywood slats to the length required and lay them across the two pieces of lipping. Pre-drill and countersink each one, then glue and screw them into place using two 18 mm x no 6 screws at both ends of each slat (see Fig 8). The end slats should be 50 mm from the headboard and footboard, with a 100 mm gap between all the others.

Chair and footstool

This style of sturdy and extremely comfortable patio chair is common throughout North America, where it is called an Adirondack chair, the name deriving from the range of mountains in upper New York State. All the timbers are simply screwed and glued together, using no joints. Start by making the footstool, and when you have gained confidence, tackle the chair.

It is possible to construct this chair from almost any timber, even 18 mm exterior-grade or marine plywood. If cost is of little concern, teak or iroko would be superb. I used secondhand mahogany; it was poor quality, had been stored in inadequate conditions, and was designated as flooring grade, but it was ludicrously cheap and basically sound.

If you feel that the sloping back of the chair is beyond your capabilities, make the chair with a 90-degree back and straight slats screwed to the back of the final seating slat, which would be straight, as opposed to the curved one shown here. To finish, I used a two-part epoxy coating. This is expensive and tricky to apply, but once wood is properly coated with epoxy, it becomes totally stable and virtually maintenance-free. Stains, polyurethane varnish and gloss paint are acceptable for the finish, but you will have to revarnish or paint your chair every four or five summers.

Essential Tools

pencil, straightedge, tape, square, marking gauge, sliding bevel, string, screwdriver, tenon saw, panel saw, jigsaw, electric drill, 3 mm, 4 mm, 6 mm and 8 mm wood bits, size 8 plug cutter, block plane, jack plane, Workmate or workbench

OTHER USEFUL TOOLS
belt sander, palm sander, beam compass, spokeshave

Chair and footstool

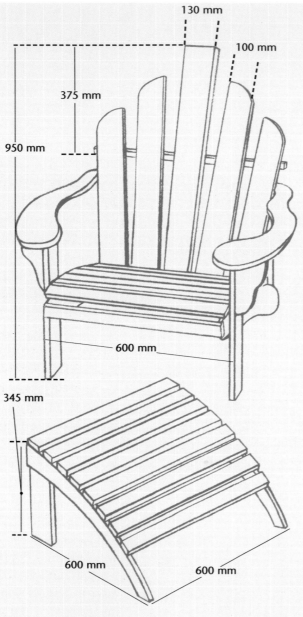

You'll need to know

ADHESIVES
p. 17

MARKING OUT
p. 18

PLANING
p. 20

CABINET SCRAPING
p. 21

SAWING
p. 22

Materials

FOOTSTOOL

9 pieces 600 x 50 x 25 mm (slats)
2 pieces 600 x 150 x 25 mm (side rails)
2 pieces 300 x 100 x 25 mm (legs)
36 zinc-plated countersink screws 38 mm x no 8
2 brass bolts 65 x 6 mm with nuts and washers

CHAIR

8 pieces 600 x 50 x 25 mm (seat slats)
2 pieces 900 x 150 x 25 mm (side rails)
2 pieces 500 x 100 x 25 mm (legs)
2 pieces 200 x 100 x 25 mm (arm rest brackets)
2 pieces 750 x 200 x 25 mm (arm rests)
700 x 170 x 25 mm (curved seat slat/back joining rib)
2 pieces 600 x 90 x 25 mm (back braces)
2 pieces 620 x 100 x 25 mm (outer back slats)
2 pieces 730 x 100 x 25 mm (inner back slats)
850 x 130 x 25 mm (centre back slat)
700 x 50 x 50 mm (strengthening blocks)
200 zinc-plated countersink screws 38 mm x no 8
40 zinc-plated countersink screws 45 mm x no 8
4 brass bolts 65 x 6 mm with nuts and washers
epoxy wood glue (system 106 or equivalent)
sandpaper grades 80 to 300

An alternative design for these chairs and stools is to use mortise and tenon joints; the method here is just as sturdy – and easier!

FOOTSTOOL

1 The upper and lower radii of the stool rails are 750 mm, with the centres taken from two different positions. Set this out first on some scrap ply or paper first. Draw a line 570 mm long, divide it in half and draw a line 55 mm at right angles to the centre. Extend the line back along the 55 mm until it is 750 mm in total. This is the position of your first centre. Set your beam compass or string and pencil accordingly and strike the upper arc (see Fig 1). Where the arc touches the 570 mm line, square off 38 mm at one end and 75 mm at the other. These two new lines give you

FIG 1

FIG 2

the position of the second centre by simply scribing an arc at 750 mm from the end of each line; where the arcs intersect is the second centre point. Cut out the shape with a jigsaw and use it as a template for the other rail. Do not cut to the 38 mm line, but leave the rail overlong at this stage. Lay each rail over the leg section, clamp them together and rest on a flat surface. Mark the base line of the rail by scribing from the table, cut and check. Mark and cut any overhang at the wider end of the rail, which needs to finish flush with the back edge of the vertical leg.

2 When you are happy that the assembly sits flat on the surface, drill and bolt the two parts together; do not overtighten. Next cut out all the slats, rounding the first slat if you wish. When they are all cut to length and arrised, lay them out together and mark out for the screw holes. Come in half the width of a rail from the end of each slat, and mark two equidistant screw holes for each end of each slat. With an 8 mm bit, drill down about 5 mm for the plugs, then drill through with a 4 mm bit for the screw shank (see Fig 2).

FIG 3

3 Fix all the slats in place one by one, 15 mm apart, using two MDF or ply spacers, drilling through the screw shank hole into the rails with a 3 mm pilot hole (see Fig 3). Fix one slat at a time and check that the two rails remain parallel and that you are fixing the slats square to the rails. Do not drive the screws fully home or glue up.

4 From offcuts matching the footstool, cut a sufficient number of plugs to fill the screw holes, using a guide for the plug cutter clamped to the wood (see Fig 4). The guide can be made from 6 mm MDF or plywood. When you have enough plugs, disassemble the stool and position the screws, nuts and bolts to hand. Ensure that the work area is dust-free and prepare to glue up (refer to step 15 for details). Before driving in the screws during final assembly, rub each screw thread against a wax candle or some beeswax to drive them home with far less effort.

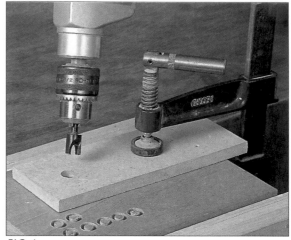

FIG 4

CHAIR

FIG 5

5 Draw out the rails freehand onto the 900 x 150 mm lengths. Use the full length, and make sure that the rails are not less than 100 mm wide at any point. The height at the front of the chair rail should match the height of the back of the footstool (about 300 mm). As you have already done for the stool, scribe the back to the bench top while the leg is clamped in position but this time, instead of cutting the front end of the rail flush to the leg, let it project forward about 100 mm and round it off. Mark the position of the leg on the rail and unclamp. Mark two flats on the front that you have drawn; these will take the front two rails, the uppermost needing to be 15 mm forward of the front of the leg. Draw the flat 50 mm, add another 15 mm gap, and then draw the second 50 mm flat (see Fig 5). Cut this out with a jigsaw and copy the shape to its pair. Finish off to a smooth surface with a belt sander and bolt the legs to the rails.

FIG 6

FIG 8

6 The top of the legs will now need to be marked and drilled for the arm rest brackets (see Fig 6). Remember to drill for the plugs first, then the shank. Drill the pilot holes when you assemble. The brackets can be a simple triangle or a little more ornate; you will get both brackets from one short length. Assemble the seat slats as in steps 2 and 3.

7 When marking out the curvature of the final seat slat, the most effective method is to use a steel rule as shown in Fig 7. As you increase the pressure at either end of the rule, you can alter the ellipse of the curve: equal pressure gives an equal curve. The timber you use should be wide enough to leave an off-cut of about 50 mm at its narrowest point; this will form the reinforcing rib behind the back. When you have decided on the amount of curvature you want for the back slats, mark and cut with a jigsaw.

8 Drill the holes for screwing the final slat to the rails and mark the centre line. Now position a flat across the curve 50 mm each side of the centre line, then use the slat spacer to mark a gap of 15 mm and after that a further 100 mm flat, as shown in Fig 8. When making the chair, I used the actual back slats as a guide from which to mark off, prior to shaping them, rather than separate guide ones. Plane to the lines of the flats and then clamp them in place on the seat assembly, checking slats and rails for square.

FIG 7

FIG 9

9 Position the offcut left over from step 7 by using the spacers, 15 mm away from the clamped slat. Use a small offcut about 25 mm thick to transfer the flats to form the front profile of the reinforcing rail for the back slats (see Fig 9). Cut to the scribed lines with a jigsaw.

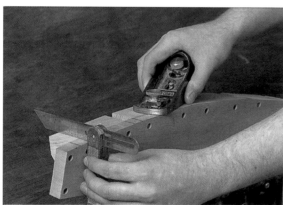

FIG 10

10 Unclamp the final slat from the assembly and screw five strengthening blocks, each about 90 mm long, to the underside, to give an added glue area to the base of the back slats. Any strong hardwood will do for the strengthening blocks; I used some offcuts of beech I had in my workshop. Screw the blocks from underneath to the rear of the final rail, running along each flat. Plane them flush using a block or a jack plane to achieve a consistent bevel of about 85 degrees, as shown in Fig 10.

11 Place the final slat edge down on the work bench and lay out the five pre-cut slats that form the back. The two 620 mm long back slats are placed at the outside, then the 730 mm slats, with the longest at 850 mm, placed in the middle. Try to get an even distance between each slat at the top. Position the offcut from step 7 about two-thirds of the way along the back to form a rib. This takes trial and error; you may find you have to reduce or increase the splay of the back, or lengthen the flats on the rib. When the fit is acceptable, mark the back slats where the rib sits and set aside. Mark each slat for the top profile and the bottom angle. Cut to fit with a jigsaw. You can copy the top detail from the photograph on page 34, if you wish.

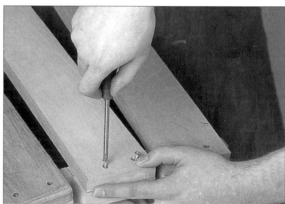

FIG 11

12 When cut, drill and screw together and place the assembly back on the rails. At this stage the back is fragile and will flop about, so take care. Check the fit of the rib again and, if good, drill through the back slats, two holes per slat, taking great care that the drill does not burst through the face of the rib. Screw the rib and back slat temporarily in place to provide some rigidity – every other screw hole will be sufficient at this stage (see Fig 11). From the narrowest point of the rib draw a smooth line that follows the curvature of the back to each end. Draw a half-round to finish level with the two end back slats. Remove, cut the waste with a jigsaw, sand or plane smooth, then refit.

FIG 12

FIG 13

FIG 14

13 Fit the two braces that support the back underneath the back rib. Bolt them to the inside of the back of the rails. Leave the bottom width of the braces at 90 mm and taper the upper end so that it is the same width as the rib. Cut the bottom as a half-round and the top as a compound mitre, meeting the back face of the outer back slat and the underside of the rib (see Fig 13 for detail). Mark the compound mitre by scribing from the relevant faces, and use a sharp block plane to plane down to the lines (Fig 12). When correctly shaped, drill and screw the top in place and use a bolt to fix the brace to the bottom to the rail.

TIP

When gluing up, cover your workbench with newspaper to catch any drips of adhesive.

---

14 The key factors influencing the shape of the arms are: at the front, you need enough space for a large gin and tonic, and the back needs to curl around the outside of the outer edge of the outer back slat and butt up to the outer face of the braces. The best way to achieve this is to use an offcut of MDF or ply and obtain the shape by a process of trial and error (see Fig 14). Use a spirit level to position the arms, then mark the underside where it meets the brace. Fit a small block at this mark and then screw the arm down onto the block. The front of the arm is screwed down into the front leg and arm rest bracket. When gluing up, pour a little glue into these holes as you are screwing into end grain.

15 When applying epoxy resin, use rubber gloves, mix accurately according to the manufacturer's instructions, and work quickly – drips and spillage can be cleaned off later. Mix only as much glue as you can use in 25 minutes. Glue the legs, rails and slats together, screwing and bolting as you go, then mix a further amount for the plugs. Leave to cure for a day, then clean off any excess glue with a chisel and sandpaper and cut the plugs flush.

Shelving unit

A fundamental of good kitchen design is the rule of conceal and display: conceal the unattractive, and display – with verve – the attractive!

This shape works best when hung between two ordinary wall units. It breaks up the rigid lines of most fitted kitchens and allows the eye to be caught by the display. The unit is designed to complement the kitchen sink and wall unit on pages 130–140. Use 12 mm board for the shelf dividers, as the difference in the thickness between the dividers and the 15 mm shelves provides a balance that works well visually. Note also that the end of the front curve passes in front of the sides; this is a bit of a fiddle to mark out, but it will give your shelves a far slicker look.

As always, wear a face mask when working with MDF, especially when working with power tools. The finish used here is eggshell paint but you could use emulsion, maybe picking out the leading edge of the shelves in a complementary tone, finishing with matt varnish.

Essential Tools

pencil, steel rule or tape, square, string, panel saw, router with 12 mm and 15 mm straight cutters, jigsaw, face mask, drill, 3 mm twist bit, screwdrivers, 12 mm bevel-edge chisel, mallet, jack plane, 2 sash cramps or cramp heads, two 300 mm G-cramps, Workmate or workbench

OTHER USEFUL TOOLS
beam compass, circular saw, cordless screwdriver, belt sander

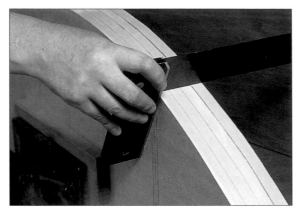

FIG 6

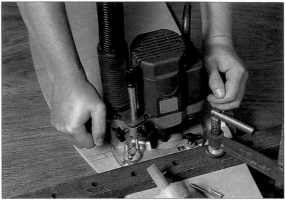

FIG 7

6 Keeping the cramps in place, release the shelves from the vice and turn them around with the curved front edges uppermost. Finish these edges with a belt sander or a sharp plane, working from each end towards the middle. As you work, check the front edges for square, correcting as necessary (see Fig 6). Release the shelves from the vice and cramps. Mark each shelf to identify it: 'top', 'upper middle', 'lower middle' and 'bottom'. The top shelf has one centrally placed housing on the underside; mark it accordingly. The upper middle shelf has one housing on the top in the centre but two offset on its underside; use one of the shelves that were on the outside when they were in the vice, as they will already have the two outer housings marked on it. Finally set your marking gauge to 20 mm and run it across the front end of each housing. The housings are 'stopped housings', so you will not see them from the front when the unit is assembled.

7 Set up your router to cut a 12 mm housing to a depth of 5 mm, and use a fence clamped to the shelf (see Fig 7). Make sure that the cramp is firmly fixed and will not move, then run the router along the fence until you reach the mark made by the marking gauge in step 6. Repeat for each housing on all the shelves.

FIG 8

8 Now cut the ends of your shelves to allow the front edge to pass over the front edge of the sides. For the middle two shelves the process is to mark a line 15 mm in from each end, square from the back of the shelves, then a second line square from the point where the arc meets the end. Remove this 100 x 15 mm portion with a hand- or jigsaw. Repeat the marking-out on the underside of the top shelf and on the top of the bottom shelf. Remove these two portions with the router to a depth of 5 mm, using a 15 mm cutter and a fence set up as before; stop when you reach the line from the end of the arc (see Fig 8).

TIPS

To ensure that you have measured the correct distance from the edge of your router baseplate to the fence, do a test cut on a piece of waste before starting to cut in earnest. To check the alignment, run the router over the cut with the cutter lowered and the motor switched off.

FIG 9

FIG 10

9 Clean up the stopped ends with a sharp chisel. Retrieve the offcut from step 1, then mark it twice to 100 x 710 mm for the sides. Cut the offcut and run a plane over the saw cuts to tidy them up. Next take the 12 mm MDF and cut the uprights: two at 300 x 230 mm and two at 260 x 230 mm. Mark and cut the waste for the stopped housings as shown in Fig 9, to 5 mm deep and 20 mm long on the top and bottom of each upright. (The 230 mm is the height.)

10 Clear your workbench and lay the shelves out in order on their back edges. One by one place the uprights in place, the deeper uprights in the centre of the top and bottom shelves, and the shallow ones offset between the two middle shelves. Place the side panels in place and get the whole assembly approximately square. Fix a batten down to the bench to hold the bottom shelf in place, fix another batten about 30 mm away from and parallel to the top shelf, then push a set of folding wedges in place. Repeat for the sides. Place your cramps and folding wedges in position with scrap wood as protection, and use them to pull everything into square. If the backs of the shelves are not sitting tight up against the uprights, use an offcut to force them together. When everything fits and is square, mark the centres of the shelf ends where they meet the sides.

11 Dismantle the assembly, square down from the marks on the side panels and drill two 3 mm holes in each line. Apply PVA glue to all joints, including the shelf ends, and reassemble. Replace the cramps, wedges and offcuts, recheck for square both internally and externally, and drive the 50 mm screws into the holes drilled in the side panels (see Fig 10).

FIG 11

12 Wipe away excess glue with a damp rag (see Fig 11), leave overnight to dry, and then release the wedges and cramps. If any screws are not driven below the surface, withdraw them, countersink the holes and drive them in again. Fill over the screw heads with filler, then plane the front of the uprights to suit the arc of the shelves, planing towards the centre. Finally, sand the edges and the filler over the screws, and paint as required. Use two mirror plates on each of the top and bottom shelves to fix the unit to the wall.

Bathroom accessories

These pieces are designed as a hardwood starter project. You need some basic skills, but not necessarily to have worked with hardwoods before. The project allows you to practise the skill of getting timber perfectly flat and of an even thickness using hand tools. It also introduces the cabinet scraper, an essential tool for obtaining a smooth surface on hardwoods. A biscuit jointer is used for the soap dish and the toothbrush holder; one can be hired for the weekend at a reasonable cost, although once you have used it and appreciated its time-saving versatility, you will want to purchase one.

Burr maple is used for the fittings and plain maple for the duckboard. Virtually any timber could be used – see what your local timber merchant has in stock – but please don't use pine, as it is the quality of the timber used that makes this set of accessories look so attractive. You must use water-resistant glue for this project, as all the items will be subject to the damp atmosphere of the bathroom. The finish is a natural beeswax polish.

Essential Tools

pencil, compasses, tape, square, crosscut saw, jigsaw with scroll blade, electric drill, 10 mm, 6 mm and 3 mm wood bits, biscuit jointer and 5 size 20 biscuits, coping saw, half-round file, 12 mm bevel-edge chisel, jack plane, block plane, cabinet scraper, Workmate or workbench

OTHER USEFUL TOOLS
table-mounted circular saw

Bathroom accessories

Your fittings may be a different size or proportion to mine, in which case adapt the sizes. The only important thing is that there should be a visual balance between the fittings and the wood.

You'll need to know

PLANING
p. 20

SAWING
p. 22

BISCUIT JOINTERS
p. 23

490 mm

42 mm

Slats 12 mm thick

6mm gap

570 mm

185 mm

50 mm

86 mm

20 mm   12 mm

175 mm

86 mm

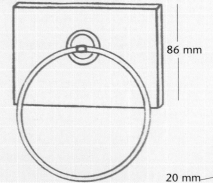

50 mm

Top face 68 mm diam hole
Bottom face 65 mm diam hole

290 mm

10 mm diam hole

86 mm

20 mm

6 mm   44 mm

16 mm

20 mm

Materials

1400 x 100 x 20 mm burr maple or similar
12,500 x 42 x 13 mm maple or similar
100 x 6 mm dowel pegs
sandpaper grades 150 to 300
water-resistant wood glue
toothbrush mugs
toilet roll holder
towel ring

Cutting List

Towel ring 175 x 86 x 20 mm
Toilet roll holder 175 x 86 x 20 mm
Soap dish 185 x 86 x 20 mm and 185 x 86 x 20 mm
Mug holder 290 x 90 x 20 mm and 290 x 95 x 20 mm
Duckboard 14 pieces 490 x 42 x 12 mm and 4 pieces
570 x 42 x 12 mm

TOILET ROLL HOLDER AND TOWEL RING

FIG 1

FIG 2

1 Cut two lengths as per the cutting list, then use a sharp jack plane to get the best face of your blocks perfectly flat (see Fig 1). Once flat, plane the best edge true and square to the first face, then mark with face and edge marks. Set a marking gauge to 20 mm and mark around the edges, then plane the other face down to the marks. Aim for fine shavings and plane with the direction of the grain at all times. When both faces are flat and parallel to each other, set your marking gauge to 86 mm, mark for the other edge and plane down to that edge.

2 When the blocks are both accurately sized, use a block plane to remove the arris around the face sides, as shown in Fig 2. Take care that you do not cause splitting when you plane across the end grain; to avoid this, plane from both ends towards the centre. You may find a sharp chisel the best method for the corners.

3 Finish off the front face with a cabinet scraper, then pre-drill pilot holes and screw on the fittings.

TOOTHBRUSH AND MUG HOLDER

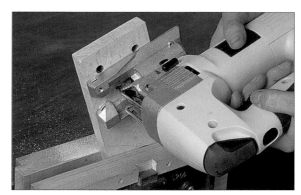

FIG 3

FIG 4

4 Prepare the timbers and mark out for the fittings. To determine the size of the holes for the tapered mugs measure the diameters of the top and the base of the mug, halve the difference between the two diameters and then add that figure to the base diameter. Draw the circles with a compass and drill a 10 mm hole in the centre for the jigsaw scroll blade (see Fig 3). Use a half-round file or rasp to clean up the jigsaw cut and to introduce the bevel needed to grip the mugs, as shown in Fig 4. Take your time and test the fit of each mug as you go.

FIG 5

5 On the back piece, mark a line about 25 mm from the bottom and run this line along the length of the back. Lay the shelf part against the back and draw three lines on both sections; these will be used as registration marks for the biscuit jointer. One line needs to be in the centre, and the other two should be approximately 50 mm in from each end. Use the biscuit jointer to cut the slots with the work held in the vice (see Fig 5). Check for fit with the biscuits in place and then glue up.

SOAP DISH

FIG 6

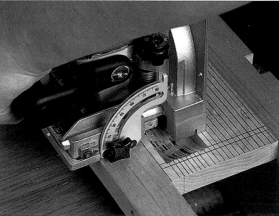

FIG 7

6 Prepare the timber as step 1, then mark out the face side as Fig 6. The multiple lines on the wood are guides for the biscuit jointer to cut out the dish by means of multiple grooves. The lines that run across the width are to line up with the registration marks on the footplate of the jointer.

FIG 8

7 If you are nervous about cutting slots accurately, practise on scrap timber first, and remember to travel in the direction of the blade, i.e. from left to right (Fig 7). Use the lines to keep the tool square, and never plunge the tool into the work until the blade has achieved full speed.

8 The width of the dish allows you to use the end of a cabinet scraper to achieve a perfect finish (see Fig 8) – take care that the corners of the scraper do not cut into the sides of the dish. To fit the back in place, repeat step 5 as described for the toothbrush and mug holder, although this time you will only need two biscuits, owing to the shorter length of the soap dish.

DUCKBOARD

FIG 9

FIG 10

9 Prepare all the lengths and lay out two long pieces with two short ones on top at the ends to make a frame. Get the four corners square and then clamp the pieces to the bench. To drill for the dowel pegs use a 6 mm drill with a tape mark as a depth gauge, as shown in Fig 9. You do not want to drill all the way through both pieces, but stop the hole about halfway through the lower piece. Drill two holes on each corner and insert pegs into the holes. The frame will now be rigid, allowing you to place the other slats equally spaced apart. Repeat the drilling at all points.

10 Cut off the protruding pegs with a coping saw (see Fig 10), cutting as close as you can but taking care not to scratch the surface. Mark the planks then disassemble, keeping each peg in its correct hole. Glue up and clamp by using lengths of stout timber clamped at each end to make a sandwich.

11 Finally use a sharp chisel to remove any excess glue from the pegs, as shown in Fig 11. You should finish the duckboard with a perfectly smooth surface, achieved by using the cabinet scraper.

TIP

When you are cutting a circular hole with a jigsaw, do not cut right up to the line. The blade can waver and you may make the cut too large on the underside.

FIG 11

Console table

This project is fairly easy to undertake, but requires the ability to cut accurate 45-degree mitres for fitting the legs to the rails. These are best cut on a table-mounted circular saw or a chop saw, but a manual mitre saw will suffice as long as you mark the mitre all the way around the timber, clamp the wood to the saw bed and take it slowly.

After cutting, the legs are smoothed with a spokeshave; a round-profile. A surform tool or rasp will do the job, but takes a little longer. A template of the leg design is shown on page 141, but I would encourage you to experiment with alternative profiles. The only thing to remember is to minimise any short grain in the profile – this means any length of timber which has been cut diagonally across the grain, leaving an area, usually a point, which can snap off if the grain at the point is short in length. The danger points are at the tip or toe of the leg and, for want of a better term, the ankle, so don't be too flamboyant in your design.

To finish, I stained the wood using a solution of instant coffee and water, which gives an attractive aged look, and then rubbed beeswax balsam over the surface.

─────────── Essential Tools ───────────

pencil, tape, combination square, screwdriver, crosscut saw, jigsaw, spokeshave, electric drill, 3 mm wood bit, countersink bit, biscuit jointer and 10 size 20 biscuits, 12 mm bevel-edge chisel, jack plane, block plane, Workmate or workbench, sash cramps and G-cramps

OTHER USEFUL TOOLS
table-mounted circular saw or chop saw, belt sander

Console table

Apart from the lipping around the edge of the table top, you can use ordinary deal timber, carefully selected for lack of knots.

**You'll need
to know**

MARKING OUT
p. 18
BISCUIT JOINTERS
p. 23
CUTTING MITRES
p. 27

Materials

2300 x 200 x 25 mm pine
or similar

3600 x 100 x 25 mm pine
or similar

3800 x 100 x 35 mm pine
or similar

3200 x 20 mm hardwood
decorative lipping

8 countersink screws
75 mm x no 10

16 countersink screws
35 mm x no 8

40 countersink screws
18 mm x no 6

8 shrinkage plates

sandpaper grades 80 to 150

PVA wood glue

approximately 30 moulding pins
20 mm long

500 mm · 1150 mm · 20 mm · 700 mm · 680 mm

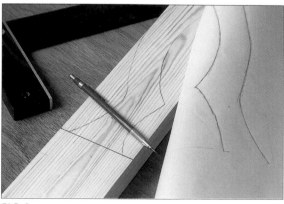

FIG 1

1 To start, you need to prepare the legs. Cut the 100 x 35 mm section timber into four equal lengths, and square each length across the ends. Measure up 680 mm and square another line around each leg. Take a tracing of the leg template on page 141, or make one of your own design, then lay it over one leg and press down the design through to the wood, reinforcing it with a pencil mark on the timber as you go (see Fig 1). Mark this leg as your pattern for shaping the other three.

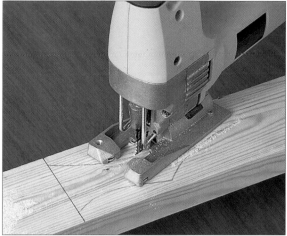

FIG 2

2 Ensure that the leg is secured to your Workmate or bench, and carefully cut out to the line with a jigsaw (see Fig 2). Saw off the excess from the length with a hand saw or circular saw, and put aside. The offcuts from the legs will form the corner blocks that secure the legs of the table to the frame.

FIG 3

3 Shape the leg with a spokeshave, Surform tool or rasp (see Fig 3). When the cut is roughly square and you are happy with the basic shape, place it on the other three leg lengths, draw around it and repeat steps 2 and 3. Finish all the legs with a belt sander or sandpaper until they are smooth and even. Do not sand the tops of the legs at this stage.

> ## TIP
> **To avoid damaging the faces of the rails when you tighten up the cramps, saw off the sharp points from the small scrap offcut blocks.**

FIG 4

4 Fig 4 shows one of the offcut blocks being cut on a table saw, with the guard removed for the sake of clarity. The short point measurement (see step 5) is the same as the width of the back of the leg. Take care when cutting the blocks as it is essential that they are true and square; save the small offcuts.

5 To measure the rails from the 100 x 25 mm timber, take the 'long points', the widest distance between two angled lines: looking down onto the wood edge, make two square lines across the edge at a given distance apart. Use the 45-degree shoulder of your combination square to make two further lines at 45 degrees running towards each other, from the same places as the two square lines. Cut two lengths mitred at 1000 mm between the long points, and two at 400 mm.

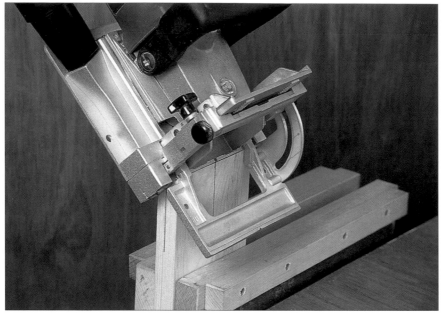

FIG 5

about one third into the mitre from the short point. Then draw a line along the mitred face and continue it onto the edges, so that you can align the registration marks on the footplate of the biscuit jointer. Clamp the rail in the vice as shown in Fig 5, set the jointer to the correct depth, then align the registration marks by adjusting the jointer's fence, and cut the slots for the biscuits (practise on some scrap beforehand). Then mark out the legs by transferring the marks from the rails onto the sides of the legs. The important thing to achieve in all this is that the short point of your rails should abut the back of the legs exactly. This is a tricky operation, so you will need to take care when you are marking out the legs.

6 Mark out the mitred ends of each rail by halving the width and carrying this mark over to the front and back faces. Then take a biscuit and find the optimum placing for the cut: it should be not too near the outside face, otherwise you will run the risk of the cutter splitting out – you should find that the best place is

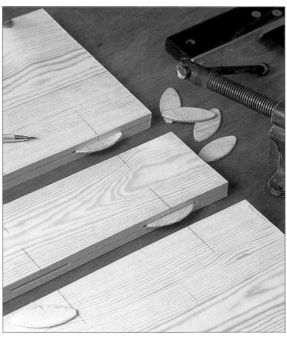

FIG 6

7 Cut the 200 mm plank into two lengths, each of 1150 mm, and the remainder of the 100 x 25 mm plank to the same length. Place the best faces uppermost and arrange them as you think best, with the 100 mm between the 200 mm planks. To minimise any warping or bowing, place the end grain of each plank in alternate directions and mark these with a face mark. The centre line of the end biscuits should be about 50 mm from the ends of the planks, with all the other biscuits about 150 mm apart. Clamp each board face side uppermost to your bench, with a slight overhang along the edge. Set the jointer to cut along the centre of the edge, and align the registration mark with your pencil lines. Check that the depth is set to size 20 and cut all the slots on the three boards. Insert the biscuits as shown in Fig 6, then glue and clamp the boards.

FIG 7

8 When the top is completely dry, turn it over and plane off any irregularities. Now check that the ends are all flush; if not, cut them square with a circular or hand saw. Assemble the legs, rails and blocks, remembering to place the biscuits in the slots as you go. In Fig 7, you will see that small blocks have been

used as packing for the clamp; these are the offcuts from the corner blocks. Drill out and countersink six holes for the screws. Drive the screws almost home, then check each corner for a square and tight fit. When you are satisfied that all the joints are good, disassemble the piece, glue up, clamp together and drive home the screws. Clean off any excess adhesive with a damp cloth and check the frame once more to ensure that it is absolutely true and square.

9 Place the edge lipping against the relevant edge and mark the short points. Cut the mitres with a tenon saw in a mitre block or in a mitre saw, and fix the edge lipping to the top, using glue and moulding pins. Clean up with a sharp chisel. When the assembly is completely dry, centre it over the upside-down table top and fix with the corner plates (see Fig 8). These have slots running in two directions, to allow movement of the top in relation to the rails. Place your screws in the middle of these slots, and use only the slot that runs parallel to the width of the top to fit the screws.

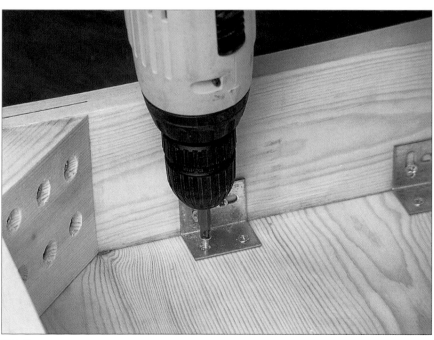

FIG 8

Birdhouse

This project is designed to be constructed with the minimum of tools and skills, although you can of course develop the basic idea. You will need to be aware of two things: first, the type of birds you wish to attract. The dimensions here are for the smaller tits; larger or more unusual birds will require different dimensions.

Second, you must make entry to the birdhouse by predators impossible. The chimney and bargeboards on the roof increase the weight, making it harder for the predator to dislodge, the extreme angle of the roof allows no footholds, and the epoxy glue coating around the entrance hole makes it difficult to enlarge the entrance hole by chewing to gain entrance.

Looking down the list of essential tools required, there is one tool that is a little specialized. A gouge is a curved chisel, mainly used in the workshop for fitting curved mouldings to a mitre. Here I used it to achieve a 'Hansel and Gretel' look on the roof tiles, but you could just as easily use a normal chisel and have rectangular roof tiles.

Paint your birdhouse with ordinary emulsion, using a crackle glaze applied between two complementary shades, and finish with two coats of exterior varnish.

Essential Tools

pencil, tape, square, sliding bevel, Stanley knife, jigsaw with scrolling blade and straight cutting blade, electric drill, 6 and 25 mm wood bits, 19 mm gouge, jack plane, block plane, Workmate, G-cramp

Birdhouse

You'll need to know

CHISELS
p. 9

ADHESIVES
p. 17

SAWING
p. 22

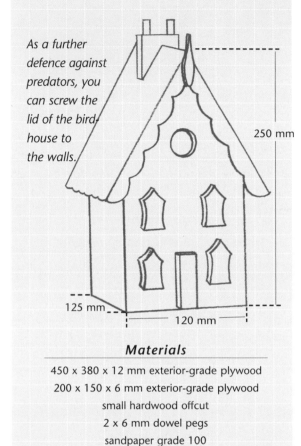

As a further defence against predators, you can screw the lid of the bird-house to the walls.

250 mm

125 mm

120 mm

Materials

450 x 380 x 12 mm exterior-grade plywood
200 x 150 x 6 mm exterior-grade plywood
small hardwood offcut
2 x 6 mm dowel pegs
sandpaper grade 100
two-part epoxy glue

Cutting list

all pieces cut from 12 mm plywood
2 pieces 220 x 120 mm (front and back)
2 pieces 100 x 110 mm (sides)
100 x 97 mm (base)
2 pieces 160 x 160 mm (roof)

FIG 2

2 To achieve the pitch of the roof, first mark a centre line through the front and back panels. Measure up from the base line of the front 110 mm to give the height of the side panels. Join the top of the centre line to the end of the 110 mm line; this gives the angle of the roof pitch. Set a sliding bevel to this angle and mark the angle on the back (see Fig 2). Cut out all the parts with a jigsaw or hand saw.

FIG 3

3 Place one of the sides of the roof in the jaws of your Workmate and plane the angle of the ridge across the grain (see Fig 3), using your sliding bevel to check that the angle is true. Repeat for the matching piece.

FIG 1

1 Referring to the diagram and cutting list above, mark out a piece of 12 mm plywood (see Fig 1). In the photograph the thicker lines are the saw cuts, otherwise known as the kerf.

FIG 4

4 Mark a line across the faces every 8 mm or so; accuracy is not of paramount importance, but try to keep the lines square and parallel. Cut along each line with a craft knife held at an angle, as shown in Fig 4. Move along about a millimetre or so and make a further cut with the knife at the opposite angle to create a V-shape groove. When all the lines are cut, brush out the waste. Mark the entrance hole to 25 mm for small tits and 28 mm for slightly larger birds.

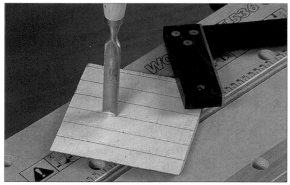

FIG 5

5 Mark out the roof tiles as shown in Fig 5. The lines are 25 mm apart, the width of a standard ruler, and the tiles are the width of the gouge. Each run is offset from its predecessor to resemble real roofing tiles. Cut the final line of tiles to its profile, using a jigsaw fitted with a scrolling blade. Drill the entrance hole using a flat bit or a hole saw. Measure and cut the chimney stack from some waste wood. Use the sliding bevel to determine the angle of the cutout, and drill two 6 mm holes in the top for the dowels.

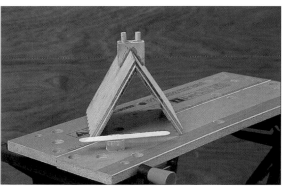

FIG 6

6 Position the chimney stack so that it acts as a simple clamp to hold the roof members together when you glue them up, as shown above in Fig 6.

FIG 7

7 Cut the fake door, windows, finial and bargeboards from the small offcut of 6 mm plywood, using a jigsaw (see Fig 7). Use some stylistic freedom here!

FIG 8

8 Glue up the house as shown in Fig 8, using one clamp to hold the box. Liberally smear a layer of glue around the entrance hole, to strengthen it against predators. Attach the bargeboards and finial to the roof assembly.

Single wardrobe

This simple project, designed to be constructed with the absolute minimum of tools and skills, is based on construction techniques used by scenic carpenters in theatre, television and films. It uses triangular plywood plates and screws to replace the more usual jointing methods. This has two advantages: one, speed of construction, and the other, the materials can be easily recycled – so when you have tired of the wardrobe or your collection of designer suits has expanded beyond its capacity, you can unscrew it, remove the ply plates and adapt or expand it as required.

The seabird finials began as flaming Olympiad torches, but were adapted to fit the brief of ease of construction. You can, of course, indulge your own design talents, but remember that whatever shape you design as a finial will be constrained by the 50 x 50 mm section of the corner posts. The sides and door are constructed from thick tongue-and-groove boards, to avoid warping and to provide sufficient thickness for the hinge. The finish is a thin emulsion wash with a dash of PVA added. Poster paints with PVA are used for the finials.

Essential Tools

pencil, tape, combination square, bradawl, screwdriver,
hammer, crosscut saw, coping saw, electric drill,
3 mm wood bit, countersink bit, Workmate

OTHER USEFUL TOOLS
jigsaw with scrolling blade, belt sander

Single wardrobe

**You'll need
to know**

IRONMONGERY
p. 16

MARKING OUT
p. 18

SAWING
p. 22

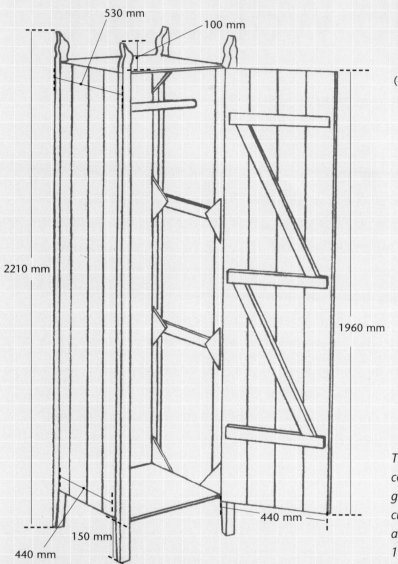

530 mm

100 mm

2210 mm

1960 mm

150 mm

440 mm

440 mm

Materials

12 pieces 2000 x 112 x 25 mm
tongue-and-grooved pine or similar
(usually sold as flooring-grade boards)

4 pieces 2300 x 50 x 50 mm pine
or similar

6500 x 50 x 25 mm pine or similar

2 pieces 500 x 500 x 9 mm ply

440 x 1960 x 6 mm ply

16 pieces 100 x 100 x 145 mm
triangular corner plates cut
from 6 mm ply

100 countersink screws
30 mm x no 6 gauge

2 magnetic catches

20 mm panel pins

handle

2 m brass piano hinge and
brass screws

20 mm dowel or brass rail

sandpaper grades 80 and 100

PVA wood glue

*The sides and door are
constructed from tongue-and-
groove boards 20 mm thick. To
cut costs, the side panels can just
as easily be constructed from 9 or
12 mm boards.*

1 To construct the sides, begin by cutting eight lengths of tongue-and-groove to 1960 mm. Select the best faces and position them in relation to each other, taking into account any warping or twist. Sort into two packs of four, slot together and plane or saw off the tongue from the end board. Cut eight 50 x 25 mm battens to the full width of the panels. Place two equidistant from the centre, and two 9 mm from the ends on each panel. Ensure that each batten lays square to the edges, and screw and glue them in place (see Fig 1). Stagger the screws and use two per board; if you are using thinner boards – for instance, 19, 12 or even 9 mm thickness – you will need shorter screws. Make sure, however, that you use 25 mm boards for the door.

FIG 1

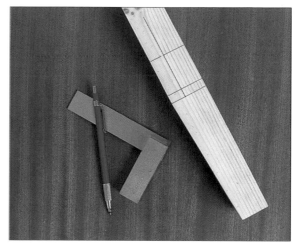

FIG 3

2 For the door, repeat step 1, except for the three battens, which will be 50 mm shorter. Place one batten in the centre of the door, one 200 mm from the top and one 300 mm from the base. The top of the door will be determined by which side will take the hinge – this has to be the edge from which you have removed the tongue. Ensure the battens lay square to the door edge, and are placed 25 mm in from the edges. Screw and glue in place as in Fig 1.

4 Mark the best two faces on each post, then mark each post as 'front left', 'rear left', etc. From the base measure up 150 mm, square round and mark a chamfer down to the base. The slope should run from the squared line taking 15 mm off the two best (outer) faces at the base of each post. Fig 3 shows a corner post with the chamfers cut. It is also marked out to show the position of the 9 mm floor of the wardrobe, the position of a side strut for the side panel and the amount of offset required when positioning the ply plates to allow the door to close. This offset will be the thickness of the door, plus 6 mm for the two front posts, but just 6 mm for the two rear posts to allow a flush fit for the 6 mm ply back.

3 To determine the length and angle required for the diagonals, place a length in position, look down from above and mark a line to cut to. Cut and screw and glue in place (see Fig 2). Cut the four corner posts to 2210 mm.

FIG 2

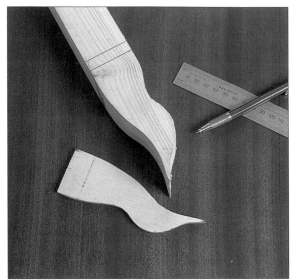

FIG 4

FIG 6

5 Mark out the position of the 9 mm ply top on the corner posts, as shown by the two parallel lines in Fig 4. The distance from the upper mark to the bottom mark should be the height of the door, ie 1960 mm. To achieve a consistent profile for the finials, cut a template from a scrap of 6 mm plyood and draw your chosen design around it. Flip the template over for the left and right corner posts. Cut the profile with a coping or jigsaw, taking care to ensure that the cut is square to the front face and that the work is well supported.

7 To fit the side panels to the corner posts, select a pair of front and rear posts and arrange them parallel to each other with the outside faces down on the bench. Lay the side panel between the posts, ensuring that the panel is at the correct height in relation to the marks you made on the posts for the top and floor. At this point, the offset that you marked in step 3 becomes particularly important. Fig 6 shows a triangular plywood plate being screwed 6 mm in from the edge of the rear post using no 6 gauge countersink screws.

6 When you have finished cutting all four finials, wrap some sandpaper around a tube of silicone or something similar and use it to smooth out the saw cut marks, as shown in Fig 5. If you have the use of a belt sander, the front end or 'nose' of the tool is quite perfectly suited for this smoothing job.

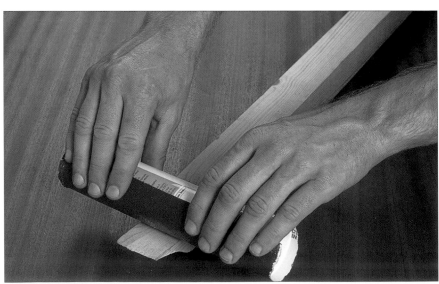

FIG 5

TIP

If you need to plane a bit from the door edge, remove the door, plane and then refit in place.

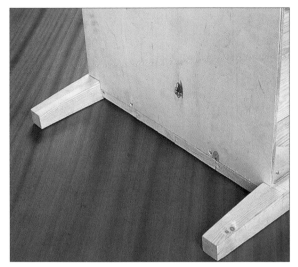

FIG 7

FIG 9

8 Use an offcut of the correct thickness to help position the plate (see Fig 7) – the thickness of the door (20 mm), plus 6 mm in from the edge of the front post. Pre-drill the plates as shown and allow the screws to pull up the side panel so that it lies flush with the upper face of the corner post.

10 Cut and true the ply to size, then cut notches at each corner to accommodate the posts. To fit the top and floor, lay one side face-down and screw the ply in place. Rotate the entire assembly through 90 degrees onto the front face and fit the other side. To fit the back, put small offcut blocks between the ply plates at the back and set them in by 6 mm, the same as the rear plates. Check the carcass is square, cut a 6 mm ply panel to fit and fix with glue and pins. Rotate the carcass again so that the hinge side is face down. Fit the door, supporting the outer edge with a small block. Fit the hinge with screws every 400 mm.

9 The dimensions of the top and floor might vary, but essentially the width will be that of the door plus the thickness of two battens, plus 2 mm for fitting the hinge. The depth will be the width of a side panel plus the thickness of two corner posts, minus the two offsets. Fig 8 shows the ply floor fitted to one side.

FIG 8

Screen

A screen is normally thought of as three or four panels connected by hinges. However, you can use as many panels as you wish – I used 24, and connected them together with rope, based on an idea I saw in Bali. In the construction I used a router table, a useful addition to the home workshop that turns your router into a small spindle moulder. It will speed up the tedious part of this project and should ensure greater accuracy in the fit of the male and female profiles.

You can use almost any timber – a maple or sycamore screen with stainless-steel cleats would look very stylish, if somewhat on the extravagant side. When selecting the timber at a yard, be firm in refusing any length that is twisted or warped, or has dry knots on either edge.

For the finish I used an interior colour wash to which I added a small amount of gold powder, available in art shops. The tassels used to hide the ends of the nylon ropes have a wooden flange on the top, through which the nylon is threaded and is then tied off under the body of the tassel.

Essential Tools

pencil, tape, square, screwdriver, tenon saw, jigsaw, electric drill, 6 mm extra-long multi-speed bit, 6 and 7 mm twist bits, 12 mm flat bit, block plane, large sash cramp or cramp heads, router mounted on router table, half-round cutter 6 mm radius, ogee cutter 6 mm radius, Workmate or workbench

Screen

You'll need to know

ROUTER TABLES
p. 12

MARKING OUT
p. 18

ROUTERS
p. 22

Although this project uses modern nylon rope and cleats, and the joining profiles have been adapted for use with a standard router cutter or spindle moulder, it is essentially the same design that has been used for hundreds of years in the Far East. Older screens of this type would have been made of what was then a plentiful supply of hardwood, but pine or a similar softwood will do just as well.

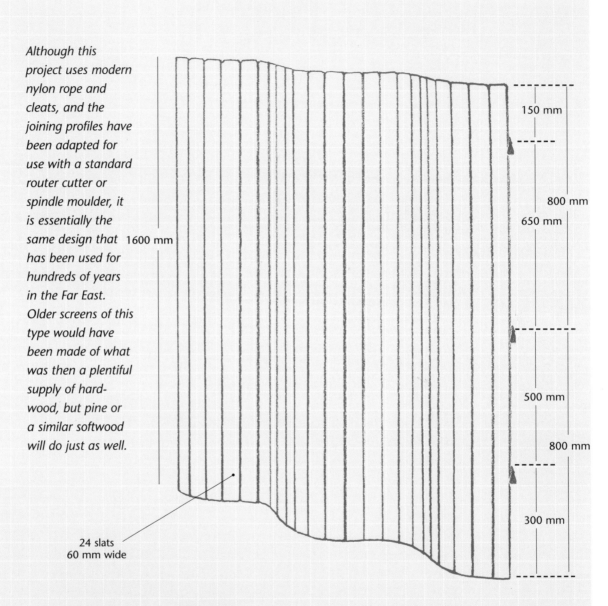

1600 mm

150 mm

800 mm

650 mm

500 mm

800 mm

300 mm

24 slats
60 mm wide

Materials

24 pieces 25 x 75 x 1600 mm straight-grained pine or similar (PAR)

5 mm diameter nylon rope, 9 m long

3 small plastic cleats

(these last two items can be bought in a chandler's or surf/dive shop)

6 screws 25 mm x no 6

sandpaper grades 80, 100 and 120

FIG 1

FIG 2

1 Cut 24 lengths of timber to 1.6 m long. Mark each length with a corresponding number (from 1 to 24) and mark a top. Number 1 will be the left-hand-side plank; make a mark on the edge halfway down, i.e. at 800 mm. Make a further mark 150 mm from the top, and another 300 mm from the base, ensuring that these marks are in the centre of the edge. Use a square to transfer these marks to the other edge. Clamp all the planks together, edge uppermost, and transfer the marks from plank 1 to all the others. Turn the pack over and repeat. Secure plank 1 in your vice and drill three 12 mm holes 12 mm deep to conceal the initial knots of the ropes, as shown in Fig 1.

2 Use a 6 mm extra-long bit to drill the holes through which the rope will pass in plank 1 (see Fig 2). Drill halfway through, keeping the bit square to the timber at all times, then drill from the other edge. If you find a slight misalignment, correct this with a small round file. A pillar drill or drill stand will speed up this process. Drill three 6 mm holes in the remaining planks.

3 Fit a 6 mm radius ovolo cutter to your router, then mount the router in the router table. Use a scrap piece to set the fence in position. Depending on the type of table you are using, the fence, in all probability, will be set at a slight angle across the centre of the cutter. The height of the cut should be to the centre line of the timber's edge, and the thickness should be so you just skim the centre edge with the cutter. The uppermost part of the profile should just touch the centre line drawn across the edge of each plank

---

TIP

If you are in any doubt whatsoever as to your competence in fusing the rope as demonstrated in step 7, you can get a good result by taping the ends with electrical tape.

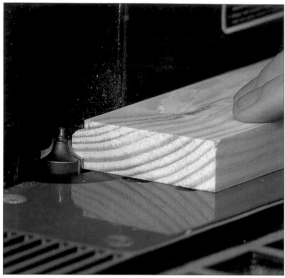

FIG 3

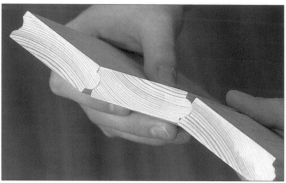

FIG 5

4 To achieve the profile, you need to make two passes, turning the timber over after the first cut (see Fig 3). When you are sure that the profile is correct, cut the edge of plank 1 that does not have the 12 mm holes drilled; this should be to the right-hand side of the plank. Then cut all the other planks on the right-hand side, except plank 24, which should be left square on the right-hand side.

5 To shape the tops, use a coin about 20 mm in diameter and place it so that it touches the top edge and the reveal of the ovolo cut. Draw around it. Place the coin against the edge and the top on the other edge, and mark. Using a jigsaw, cut square through the ovolo profile to the lines. Change the cutter in the router to a half-round with a 6 mm radius. Again, use a test piece to position the fence and the height of the cutter, then make the cut (see Fig 4).

6 Fig 5 shows in detail how the two profiles should match. Pass the left-hand side of all planks, except plank 1, through the router. Lay all the planks in order on the workbench.

7 Cut the rope into three equal lengths. Nylon rope will fray at the ends unless taped or fused. The best method is to fuse the ends together with the flame from a cigarette lighter. Make a clean cut while the rope is held taut. Take the new end and twist the rope in the direction that it falls. Run the flame of a cigarette lighter under the rope about 50 mm away from the end you are holding. Rotate the rope round and move the lighter over a 20 mm section. As soon as you can see the outer surface fusing together, remove the flame and cool the rope in water.

FIG 4

FIG 6

FIG 7

8 Make a new cut in the middle of the section you have fused together. This process needs to be done at both ends of all three ropes. Tie a figure-of-eight knot at one end (see Fig 6), to act as a stopper in the 12 mm holes in plank 1.

9 Starting from plank 1, thread each rope through one plank at a time (see Fig 7). Twist the rope with the lay, and if you find a hole tight, ream it out with a 6 mm drill bit. Push each plank up tight as you work.

FIG 8

TIP

When routing the planks, take it slowly and keep a firm pressure downwards. You may find it easier to enlist the help of an assistant to draw the planks from you as they come off the table.

10 Use a large sash cramp to pull the planks together. Screw a plastic cleat just under each hole, pulling the ropes as tight as you can, and lock them off in the cleats (see Fig 8). Offer up the tassels, if used; cut and fuse the ropes to the shortest possible length, then place the tassels in position, fixing them with glue or cotton binding.

Waney shelves

'Waney' or 'waney edge' means timber with the bark attached to one or more faces. I used fine walnut here, but I have also made similar shelving using long, straight planks with a waney surface on the front edge.

Cutting and finishing the shelves is not difficult; the cunning bit is the hidden wall fixing. I used 10 mm diameter stainless steel rods inserted in the back edge, and then car body filler to fix into both the shelf and the wall. If fitting into a corner, a nylon connecting block can be recessed into the edge to provide additional support. This method is fairly straightforward if you are fixing to a brick or stone wall, but if you live in a timber-framed house or you want to hang these shelves from a stud partition wall, a different approach must be taken.

Remove the plaster or dry wall lining from the fixing areas, from the other side of the wall. Drill through the exposed timber uprights with a 10 mm drill, insert 10 mm threaded rods, fix the rods into the shelf with body filler and when dry, tighten up the nuts from the other side and cut the rods flush to the nut's surface. Plaster over the holes and make good.

Essential Tools

pencil, straightedge, tape, square, spirit level, half-round file, electric drill, 10 mm wood bit, 9 mm masonry bit, jigsaw, jack plane, block plane, cabinet scraper, Workmate or workbench

OTHER USEFUL TOOLS
router with straight cutter (if fitting connecting block side support)

Waney shelves

Check the angle at which your walls meet first – they may not be at right angles.

Third cut

Second cut

First cut

Materials

Hardwood with an interesting grain and at least one waney edge. It will need to be purchased with a specific site in mind, and this will determine the length and width, but the finished thickness should be about 25 to 35 mm

10 mm diameter stainless steel rod, about 200 mm for every fixing point

Two-part 'elastic' car body filler

Sandpaper grades 60 to 240

You'll need to know

MARKING OUT
p. 18

CABINET SCRAPING
p. 21

ROUTERS
p. 22

1 Select the board, assess the most advantageous shape to cut and mark it out carefully. This triangular piece had a waney edge on both edges, with a sawn edge to the right-hand side. I cut across the grain at the wider end. If the shelves are to be part of a set when fixed, consider the overall shape, the direction and colouring of the grain and, most importantly, the curves and edge bevels.

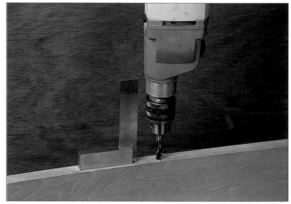

FIG 2

3 Drill 10 mm diameter holes along the back edge of each shelf – around 300–400 mm between each centre should be sufficient. The rods need to go into the shelf at least 100 mm deep. Use a square to assist you in keeping your drill perpendicular (see Fig 2), and if your shelf is tapered, be careful to avoid breakout on the front edge where the shelf narrows.

FIG 1

2 Slice off the bulk of the bark with a chisel, and use a belt sander with a coarse belt to rapidly remove all the remaining fibrous matter, or phloem (see Fig 1). You can use the nose of the tool to follow the undulations of the timber. Plane the straight edges and the two faces and finish them with a cabinet scraper as normal.

TIP

To ensure that the shelves will fit when cut, make a small card model at 1:10 or 1:12 scale beforehand.

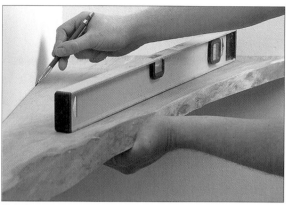

FIG 3

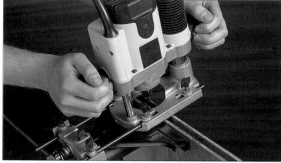

FIG 5

4 Scribe the shelves to get an exact fit up to the wall. This is particularly important if you decide to use a support method as outlined on page 77. The greater the area of contact with the wall, the better your fixing will be. Use a spirit level when marking the wall, and then use this line to scribe to (see Fig 3). At the same time, mark a further line on the wall for the underside of the shelf.

6 If you are fitting the shelves in an alcove or a corner, a way to achieve even greater hidden support is to rout out a channel in the side edge of each shelf. This should be of sufficient width and depth to receive half a nylon connector block. Start the channel about 80 mm from the back of the shelf, and stop it just short of the front (see Fig 5).

FIG 4

7 Insert the rods into the back edge and carefully mark the wall between the upper and lower lines. Drill out the wall using an undersized bit, in this case 9 mm for a brick wall; concrete or stone will require a full-sized 10 mm bit.

FIG 6

5 Each steel rod should be 10 mm shorter than the hole drilled into the back edge of your shelves, plus a minimum of 100 mm into the wall. The deeper you can fix into the wall, the better, as the shelf will be stronger. Attach your drill to a bench vice, insert the rods and use a file as shown to round off each end slightly (see Fig 4). Also cut a 'key' along the length of each rod. This will assist the filler in bonding with the stainless steel.

8 Mark for the connector block, if used. It needs to be sited the length of the protruding rods, plus 10 mm forward from the back wall. The rods can then be inserted into the wall, and when the shelf is pushed back into place, the nylon block will slide along its channel until the shelf is fully in place (see Fig 6). Hammer home the rods. Coat the wall, the protruding rods and the back edge and holes of the shelf with filler and push the shelf home. Do a dry run, and only apply the filler when you are sure all fits. Clean off any excess filler with a sharp knife before it has set fully.

Kitchen accessories

Hardwood offcuts are never discarded in my workshop. Years ago, I remember the taciturn owner of a woodyard, who, when I asked him if he had any scraps of hardwood I could have, grunted 'Ain't no such thing as scrap hardwood!' Now, I realise he was right. Here are two projects that utilise offcuts. In both, the dimensions are to some degree flexible, depending on what you have to hand.

The chopping board is designed to be a mini version of a butcher's block, with end grain uppermost. Every block within the outer frame is a regular cross section cut from various odd lengths. If you wish to follow the herringbone arrangement illustrated, this regularity is essential. However, you can create a pattern of random widths all glued up together. The frame is dovetailed together using a single pin with an angle of 1:8. This is a simple joint, but requires a fair degree of accuracy and concentration. For the knife rack (shown on page 84), I used two contrasting timbers separated by 6 mm plywood fillets. I finished the chopping board with olive oil (you could use any vegetable oil), and the knife rack with Danish oil.

Essential Tools

pencil, tape, square, sliding bevel, tenon saw or
dovetail saw, crosscut saw, bevel-edge chisel, coping
saw, jigsaw, electric drill, 4 mm wood bit, countersink
bit, jack plane, block plane, cabinet scraper, Flexicurve
or French curves, Workmate or workbench, G-cramps

OTHER USEFUL TOOLS
table-mounted circular saw, belt sander,
electric hand plane

Chopping board

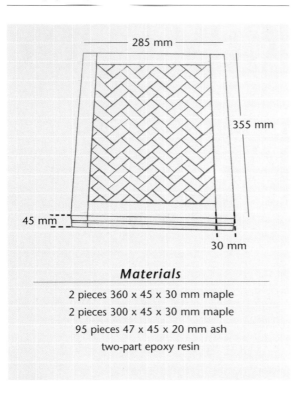

285 mm

355 mm

45 mm

30 mm

Materials

2 pieces 360 x 45 x 30 mm maple

2 pieces 300 x 45 x 30 mm maple

95 pieces 47 x 45 x 20 mm ash

two-part epoxy resin

You'll need to know

MARKING OUT
p. 18

SAWING
p. 22

SIMPLE JOINTS
p. 25

FIG 1

1 Collect together short lengths of timber of the same section, about 45 x 20 mm; you will need about 4.5–5 m in total. Saw these accurately to 47 mm, ensuring that there are no defects near either end (see Fig 1). Arrange them in rows of 12 in a herringbone pattern to create the main block. Cut two lengths of softwood batten 150 mm longer than the length of your assembled block and two lengths about 10 mm less than the width of the block.

FIG 2

2 Arrange the blocks, battens and cramps as shown in Fig. 2, then lay a sheet of newspaper over your bench and quickly apply some epoxy glue to all four faces of each block. Place the battens and clamps in place and tighten. If any outer block tends to pull away from the main body, adjust the position or tightness of the nearest cramp head, or force a small wedge of timber into the side of the batten to correct the error. Scrape off any excess glue and clean up. When the glue has dried, plane one face flat and mark a square area, using the maximum amount of the block (see Fig 7 on page 84); it may be a good idea to allow a 2 mm margin of error in from the extreme edge of the block as it's far easier to plane the edge of the block than have to re-cut dovetail shoulders. This marked area will be the inside dimension of your frame. Prepare the frame parts and transfer the marks from the block to give the shoulders of the dovetails.

3 Mark out for the dovetails: square the shoulder marks round, then square round a second line the thickness of the timbers (30 mm) out from the shoulder line. You will have some excess length, called 'horns'. Set a sliding bevel to a 1:8 slope – measure a line 80 mm long on scrap wood, then mark a second line running square to the first 10 mm long and join the two lines with a diagonal to give a 1 in 8 bevel. For the pins, set a marking gauge to 10 mm and mark a point in from the edge on the second line drawn. Repeat at both ends, front and back, and on both short lengths.

FIG 3

FIG 4

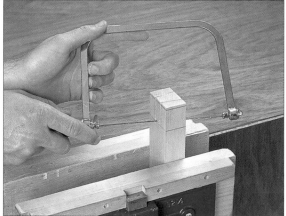

FIG 5

4 Use the sliding bevel with the stock against the narrow face to draw a line intersecting the 10 mm point down to the shoulder line. Repeat back and front and both ends. Join the bevels across the end grain and mount the timber vertically in a vice. Saw just to the outside of your bevel lines, keeping the saw level. As you approach the shoulder line, check the back to ensure that you don't cut too deep. Turn the work to a horizontal position and cut to the shoulder line, just leaving the line in place (see Fig 3).

5 Mark out the sockets in the same fashion on the longer lengths: the stock of the sliding bevel will lie against the narrow edge as before, but this time the blade runs across the end grain. Use the marking gauge at 10 mm to run from the end grain down to the shoulder line, and reset it to the thickness of the narrowest width of the peg, about 17 mm. Run this line down to the shoulder. Prior to cutting the sockets, lay all four lengths out on the bench and check that you have marked them correctly.

TIP

Coping saws are difficult to control, owing to the narrowness of the blade, so check the cut continuously.

---

6 Mount the work vertically in the vice or Workmate jaws and saw down to the shoulder lines as shown in Fig 4.

7 Remove the waste with a coping saw, as shown in Fig 5, taking care not to go too close to the shoulder line. Whatever you leave will have to be removed with a chisel later. Check the back shoulder line repeatedly as you saw.

8 Use a sharp bevel-edge chisel to remove the remaining waste. Only chisel to just past the middle of the socket, then turn the work around and come in from the other side. Keep the tool level, and don't attempt to remove too much in one go. If you encounter any resistance, give a light tap with a mallet – don't use the palm of your hand!

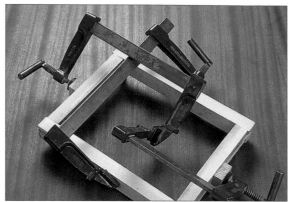

FIG 6

9 When all the joints have been cut, try a dry run. You may need to pare a small amount from the pins or the shoulders; if so, take the wood off with a chisel, a shaving at a time. When fitting the joints, do not force them in any way or you run the risk of splitting the sockets. When you have a perfect fit, lay the work on a flat surface and prepare to glue up (see Fig 6). If your cramps are too short, use two in line. When dry, saw off the horns; take care not to mark the surface.

FIG 7

10 Scrape any glue residue from the inside the frame and lay it over the main block. Check for fit, then saw the waste from the block, using a jigsaw, hand saw or circular saw (see Fig 7). Adjust if necessary by planing the edge and the back face of the block, using a belt sander fitted with a flat sanding plate and finishing with a block plane. Glue the block inside the frame, using a liberal coating of glue. When dry, use a block plane on the end grain of the dovetails. Plane off a 2 mm arris from all sharp edges.

Knife rack

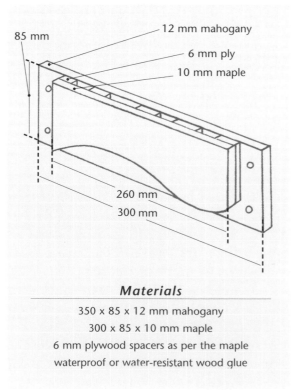

85 mm

12 mm mahogany
6 mm ply
10 mm maple

260 mm
300 mm

Materials

350 x 85 x 12 mm mahogany
300 x 85 x 10 mm maple
6 mm plywood spacers as per the maple
waterproof or water-resistant wood glue

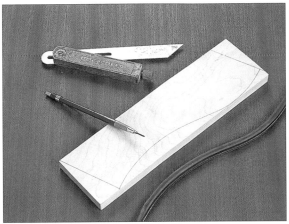

FIG 8

11 Prepare the maple front and mahogany back as per the cutting list. Mark up by setting the bevel to 20 degrees and laying the stock across the end. Draw a curve freehand or by using a Flexicurve (see Fig 8) or French curves, then cut with a jigsaw fitted with a fine blade. Use the maple as a template to copy the shape onto the plywood, and cut it out. The mahogany back needs a bevel at each end only.

FIG 10

13 Lay the plywood over the back, spacing the knives as you go, as shown in Fig 10. Mark the outlines with a pencil. Using waterproof wood adhesive according to the manufacturer's instructions, glue up the workpiece as a sandwich. Clamp up using one centrally placed large G-cramp or two equally spaced smaller ones, checking continually that none of the plywood spacers has slipped.

FIG 9

12 Lay the plywood on the back and position all the knives that you intend to use in position. Use a sharp pencil to draw around them accurately, leaving a gap of approximately 0.5 mm from the blade (as shown in Fig 9). Make sure that you identify the waste wood by crosshatching to avoid confusion, and then cut the plywood into strips.

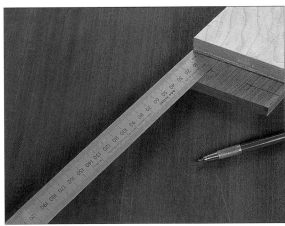

FIG 11

14 Leave the assembly to dry, preferably overnight. When it is completely dry, mark out four equally spaced 3 mm screw holes, using a ruler as a guide for spacing, as shown in Fig 11. Drill the holes, using a countersink bit, and tidy the edges up if necessary. Finally drill wall holes, insert wall plugs and screw the rack to the wall at a 20-degree angle.

Stacking storage units

A simple method of securely jointing the thin boards used in this project is to use finger joints. These are castellations running along the end of one board, with a similar set cut into the adjacent board. For the better equipped workshop, especially if you see yourself wanting to make any quantity of lightweight plywood furniture or storage boxes, I recommend you invest in a template cutter; this project uses a finger joint template. With a template such as this it is possible to cut two boards of up to 300 mm wide at once, ranged side by side; however, for the sake of clarity I've shown it being used just on one side. When you have mastered this simple jointing technique the possibilities are endless, enabling you to make a wide range of modern furniture simply, quickly and perhaps profitably!

The internal dimensions will be governed by what you intend to store: the antiqued baskets shown opposite can be obtained in a wide range of sizes. But a further consideration could well be the dimensions of your stereo or video, etc. Just draw out the external dimensions of the items, add 5 mm on each side, top and bottom, and twice the thickness of the ply to obtain the outside dimensions of the unit.

Essential Tools

pencil, steel rule or tape, square, marking knife, circular saw, router with 8 mm and 9.5 mm straight cutters, dovetail cutting jig with finger-jointing plate to suit your router, 6 mm and 9 mm bevel-edge chisels, jack plane, block plane, sash cramps, Workmate or workbench

Stacking storage units

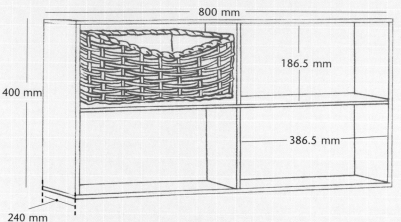

800 mm

400 mm

186.5 mm

386.5 mm

240 mm

When working with plywood, it is essential to guard against splitting or breaking out of the surface. Before each cut or router pass, score the top surface with a craft or marking knife.

You'll need to know

MATERIALS
p. 14

MARKING OUT
p. 18

ROUTERS
p. 22

Materials for three units

2440 x 1220 x 9.5 mm birch-faced plywood (boxes)
1220 x 800 x 6 mm MDF or plywood (backs)
PVA wood glue
20 mm moulding pins
sandpaper grades 100 and 150

Cutting list per unit

2 pieces 800 x 240 x 9.5 mm (top and base)
2 pieces 400 x 240 x 9.5 mm (sides)
790 x 234 x 9.5 mm (middle shelf)
2 pieces 234 x 194.5 x 9.5 mm (shelf dividers)
791 x 391 x 6 mm (back)

FIG 1

FIG 2

1 The most economical method of cutting a sheet of ply to the cutting list is to cut the top, sides and the middle shelf all running across the board, with the shelf dividers then taken from the waste. Mark and cut each component one by one. Before cutting, use a sharp knife to score the face of the board with two parallel lines the width of the kerf. Clamp a straight length of timber securely to the board as a guide fence for the saw, as shown in Fig 1.

2 Sort the sides, bottoms and tops of the unit into groups. On the inside faces of each piece, mark the shoulders of the finger joints using the adjacent component as a guide (see Fig 2). Repeat this process for all the joints.

FIG 3

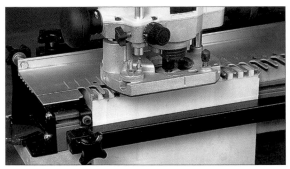

FIG 5

3 Fit the finger-jointing template in place of the normal dovetail one, inserting a block of MDF to prevent the rear of your work splitting (see Fig 3). This block must be square and true on the front edge and should be placed in line with the cut line on the template surface. The smaller piece of MDF in the foreground will keep the template flat.

4 Clamp the template to the bench with a slight overhang at the front. Fit the 11 mm guide plate (supplied with the template) and an 8 mm straight cutter to your router. Mount the work, ensuring that the upper surface is perfectly aligned with the top of the anti-breakout block and that the work is clamped securely. Use the fine adjuster on the router to lower the cutter exactly to the pencil line drawn in step 2. Rout out all the top and base parts at both ends, working left to right.

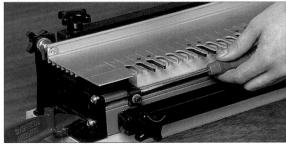

FIG 4

5 The template comes supplied with two 8 mm stop pins. These shift the work over 8 mm, thereby allowing the pins and sockets of the finger joints to line up. Insert the stop pins with a screwdriver (see Fig 4), then fit and cut the side panels as for the top and bottom.

6 Sort the sides, tops and bottoms into separate sets and plane the front and rear edges clean. Use the 8 mm straight cutter in your router and fit a fence set to cut a rebate 6 mm wide on the rear edge, inside face for the back (see Fig 5). The rebate should be 5 mm deep and must stop just short of the pencil lines marked in step 2. Use a 6 mm chisel to square the ends of the rebate to the line.

FIG 6

7 Ascertain the centre of the middle shelf, the top and the bottom shelves. Scribe two lines 9 mm apart with a knife and, using a fence as shown in Fig 6, rout out the rebate to take the vertical shelf dividers. The depth of cut for the top and bottom is 5 mm. For the middle shelf, cut only to 3 mm on either side. Clean up the rebates with a chisel. Assemble flat on the bench, check for fit and square, adjust as required, then glue up. For speedy finishing, the use of a belt sander is recommended. Check the internal measurements for the back, cut 6 mm plywood to fit and fix in place with moulding pins.

Corner cabinet

This corner cupboard with pierced doors is an exercise in cutting simple joints. It uses what is probably the most basic joint of all, the corner halving, made by cutting halfway through the thickness of the timber with a tenon saw and then removing the waste with a chisel. The outer surface of the wood is left just a little rough, giving the piece a rustic, cottagey feel.

The beading along the top is called 'egg and dart'. To fit this type of beading correctly will entail some complicated setting-out, so you may wish to replace this with a plain bead of similar size. The piercing can also be simplified. If you wish the piercing to be symmetrical and have both a left and right hand, use a MDF template as a stencil to transfer the design to your doors and flip the template to get both the left and right hand sides.

I painted the cupboard with a coat of rust emulsion then overpainted with jade, which I rubbed with fine wire wool to reveal a hint of the underlying colour. The brass handles and hinges are complemented by the gold paint on the inner faces of the piercing.

Essential Tools

pencil, tape, combination square, sliding bevel, screwdriver, hammer, mallet, crosscut saw, tenon saw, jigsaw with scroll blade, electric drill, 3 mm, 4 mm and 8 mm wood bits, countersink bit, 25 mm bevel-edge chisel, jack plane, block plane, Workmate, G-cramps

OTHER USEFUL TOOLS
table-mounted circular saw, belt sander, electric planer

Corner cabinet

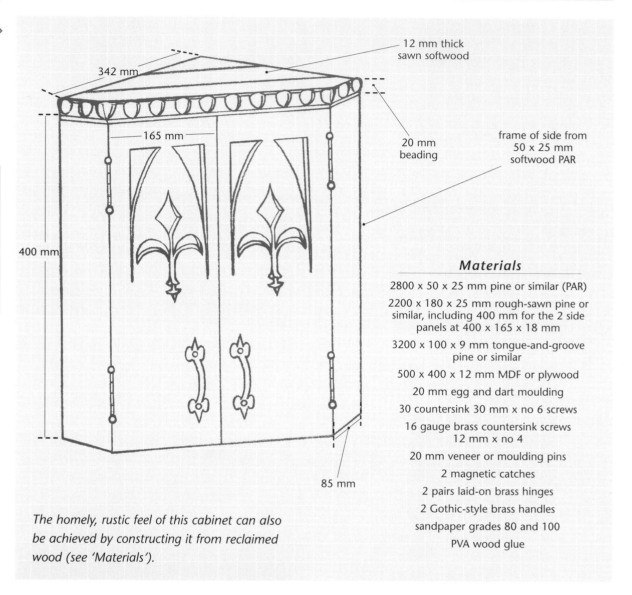

342 mm

12 mm thick
sawn softwood

165 mm

20 mm
beading

frame of side from
50 x 25 mm
softwood PAR

400 mm

85 mm

*You'll need
to know*

PREPARING TIMBER
p. 19

SAWING
p. 20

SIMPLE JOINTS
p. 25

Materials

2800 x 50 x 25 mm pine or similar (PAR)

2200 x 180 x 25 mm rough-sawn pine or
similar, including 400 mm for the 2 side
panels at 400 x 165 x 18 mm

3200 x 100 x 9 mm tongue-and-groove
pine or similar

500 x 400 x 12 mm MDF or plywood

20 mm egg and dart moulding

30 countersink 30 mm x no 6 screws

16 gauge brass countersink screws
12 mm x no 4

20 mm veneer or moulding pins

2 magnetic catches

2 pairs laid-on brass hinges

2 Gothic-style brass handles

sandpaper grades 80 and 100

PVA wood glue

*The homely, rustic feel of this cabinet can also
be achieved by constructing it from reclaimed
wood (see 'Materials').*

FIG 1

1 Make two frames from 50 x 25 mm sections of deal, with the outside dimensions of one frame 280 x 400 mm, and 300 x 400 mm for the other. Cut four lengths at 400 mm, two at 280 mm and two at 300 mm, and mark the width of the timber on the faces at the ends of all lengths and half the width, using a marking gauge. Cut the corner halving joints as shown in Fig 1. Glue up and clamp each frame, ensuring that they are square.

> **TIP**
>
> As a way of ensuring that each of the 50 x 25 mm frames are square before gluing and screwing them together, clamp each frame to the corner of the Workmate.

FIG 2

2 Join the two frames together, using the edge of your Workmate to ensure that they are square (see Fig 2). The wider frame overlaps the other, giving an equal length. Glue and screw using three 30 mm screws.

FIG 3

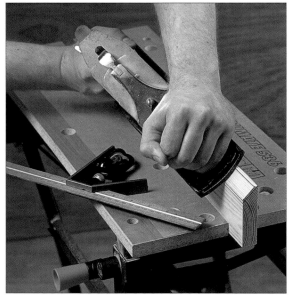

FIG 4

3 Prepare the sawn timber. You need two doors at 400 x 165 x 18 mm, two side panels at 400 x 85 x 20 mm, one top at 170 x 330 x 12 mm and the other top at 130 x 490 x 12 mm. The idea is to keep some of the rough quality of the timber, but not so much as to give you splinters; a belt sander run along the face is the best method, as shown in Fig 3. To plane down the rear face of the timbers, use an electric plane – don't plane the front faces!

4 Plane a 45-degree bevel on the inner edges of the side panels; this bevel is fixed to the hinges. Measuring from the back of each panel, the bevel needs to be in excess of the thickness of the doors: 22 mm is a good dimension, and will leave a small flat as shown in Fig 4. The hinge pin sits up to this flat. Screw the sides to the frames, recessing the screws a little. If you wish, you can fill in these screw holes prior to painting the cabinet.

FIG 5

FIG 6

5 Sit the assembly over the MDF to form the base of the cupboard. Draw around the inside of the frame (see Fig 5). When you draw inside the side bevels, take your line up to the small flat at the front of the bevel on each side and join these two points with a straight edge. Check the base for square and ensure both sides are equal, as this base will govern the finished shape of the cupboard. Cut out the shape you have drawn and finish off with a plane. Place the side and frame assembly up to the MDF and check the fit. Butt up the doors from the small flat on the side panels, sitting them on the MDF.

6 Reach inside the cupboard and mark the position of each door at the hinge edge. Join the marks with a straightedge. Make sure you are accurate, otherwise the doors will not meet correctly when closed. Cut to the line, plane true and then screw the frame assembly to the MDF. Line the inside of the frames with the tongue-and-groove lengths; start at one corner and work forward, nailing each length once the entire side has been fitted (see Fig 6). The final length on each side will need to be cut along its length to suit.

FIG 7

7 Take the two parts for the top, the wider being to the rear of the top. Place it on the cupboard and mark the 45-degree angles from the underside. Cut and screw down to the frame. The front part of the top is a little more complicated, as it needs to be cut as a lozenge shape, as shown in Fig 7. It butts up to the other part of the top and is flush to the frame at the back, but has an overhang of 20 mm at the sides and the front. The join of the beading should be at a proper place in the design, allowing the pattern of the beading to continue uninterrupted as the mitres are made.

8 Take a length of beading and cut a 67.5 degree mitre with the front of the cut in the centre of one of the darts. Hold this length up to the front of the top and choose a further dart centre at the far end. Cut back at 67.5 degrees from this new point. The short points at the rear of the beading will determine the length of the front of the top, hence the overhang, which you should duplicate for the overhang of the sides.

FIG 8

8 Fit the beading to the top with moulding pins, leaving an upstand to form a false cornice (see Fig 8). Fit the hinges to the sides at regular spacing, try the doors in place, and adjust as required by planing. There should be a gap all around the doors of about 1 mm.

9 When the doors fit, cut a template from some MDF (above right). Cut out the template with a jigsaw, ensuring the edges are square and smooth (Fig 9). Place the template over the door and spray on some paint, making sure that you get into all the corners. Flip the template and spray the other door. Cut both doors with a jigsaw. Sand off excess paint. Hang the doors, fit the handles and catches. Fill all screw holes with filler, and paint.

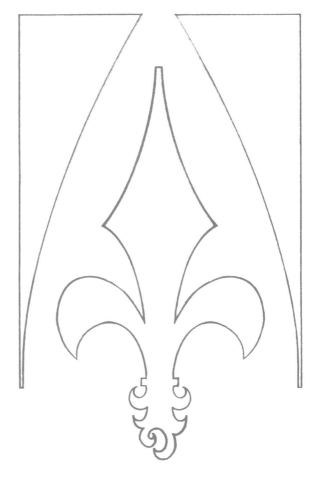

This template for the cutout on the doors is shown here slightly over half-size. Make sure that any variations match the dimensions of the doors.

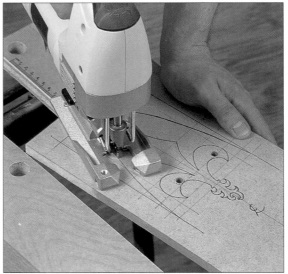

FIG 9

95

Picture rail shelf

This simple shelving system can be fixed to the walls of a room by wall plugs and screws, giving you a fashionable display and storage space that is quick and easy to construct. The height will vary according to the ceiling height of your room, but about 300 mm above head height would be normal. It may also be fixed at dado rail height, about 800 mm from the floor.

Normally, the shelf would be fixed around all the walls, with breaks for any windows or doors. When measuring the length you'll need to take into account any external mitres that need to be cut; in a modern house the rooms are usually rectangular, with no external mitres required, but in older houses you may have a chimney breast protruding into the room, which will require a mitre on either side. All the internal angles are simple butt joints. The pegs are fixed at 300 mm centres here, but they can be at any regular spacing. Note that the pegs are slightly angled upwards, at 80 degrees to the face of the support, to stop things falling off them.

The timber is softwood that is then primed and undercoated prior to fixing, and is finished with eggshell paint when in place.

—————————— Essential Tools ——————————

pencil, tape, combination square, sliding bevel,
screwdriver, mitre saw, electric drill, 25 mm hole saw
or flat bit, 4 mm wood bit, countersink bit, 25 mm
bevel-edge chisel, mallet, block plane, Workmate or
workbench, spirit level

Picture rail shelf

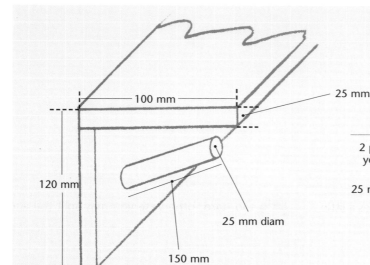

100 mm

25 mm

120 mm

25 mm diam

150 mm

Inspired by the simple, elegant designs of Shaker craftsmen, this rail can be used anywhere.

Materials

2 pieces 100 x 25 mm x the circumference of your room plus 10 per cent straight-grained pine or similar (PAR)

25 mm diameter broomstick or hardwood dowel

50 mm x no 8 countersink screws

PVA wood glue

sandpaper grades 80 and 150

small off-cuts of hardwood for wedges

You'll need to know

DRILL BITS
p. 10

PLANING
p. 20

CUTTING MITRES
p. 27

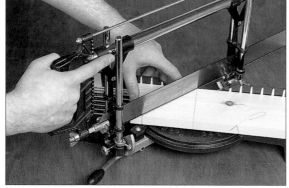

FIG 1

1 Cut the 100 x 25 mm timber into two lengths, one for the shelf and one for the support. When calculating the lengths, start in one corner of the room and work your way around. The first support will be the full extent of the wall, but subsequent ones will be shorter by the thickness of the proceeding one; the shelf measurement will also reduce by the width of the preceding one. The easiest method of cutting a mitre is to mark the actual length of the wall on the shelf, taking into account any reduction, then square across the timber and mark the mitre along the face using a combination square. Cut using a mitre saw (Fig 1) or a mitre block and tenon saw.

2 Transfer the measurement, allowing for the different reduction, to the matching support part and cut as demonstrated before.

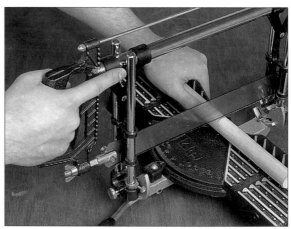

FIG 2

3 Calculate the number of pegs and cut one to length (see Fig 2). Measure this one, mark it for use as your pattern, then use the pattern as a template. I cut the pegs to 150 mm, which projects past the front of the shelf, but you can cut yours shorter, giving you more pegs per length of dowel. It is probably inadvisable to make the pegs any shorter than 80 mm.

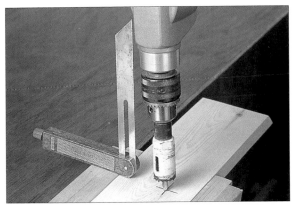

FIG 3

4 Mark out the position of the pegs at your chosen centres, with the hole centres a little below the centre line of the face side. Hold a peg in place and visually adjust the angle that you want the peg to incline. Check that you will have enough space to clear the underside of the shelf; 35 mm is an average. Secure the workpiece, use a sliding bevel set to the angle of incline of the pegs as a guide, and then drill the peg holes (see Fig 3) using a hole cutter or a flat bit drill. As you drill, be careful of any splitting out at the back.

FIG 5

6 Be careful that you do not tap the wedges too hard, otherwise you may split the end grain of the peg further than the face of the support. Leave the glue to dry, preferably overnight, then use a saw to cut the peg and wedges almost flush with the rear face. Finish by planing the peg and wedges flush to the back of the support with a block plane (see Fig 5). As always when planing end grain, apply pressure to the toe of the block plane and make sure that the blade is very sharp before you start.

FIG 4

5 Smear each peg with a little glue and insert it into the hole. Let the peg pass through the back of the support until the lower edge just meets the rear face. Ensure that the peg is supported underneath and sharply tap the end grain with a chisel. This will split the peg, allowing you to knock in a small, shallow hardwood wedge, as shown in Fig 4.

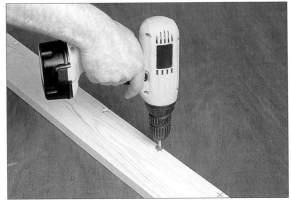

FIG 6

7 Drill and countersink the shelf components through the back edge at a regular centre of about 400 mm (see Fig 6). Match each shelf to its support, glue along the edge of the support and fasten with 50 mm screws. Keep the two parts together at 90 degrees, and be careful that the screws do not come through the face or the back of the support. Sand lightly, then prime.

Coffee table

This table is very much a modernist design, with the only decoration being in the materials. Note that the tapered legs have a line in the grain which runs through all four legs and is ranged in the same direction. It is this attention to detail that can enhance your own furniture. The proportions are of paramount importance here, and the design will not respond well to adaptation unless the whole balance is reworked.

When I first drew up this design I was a little concerned about the method used to join the legs to the top. Would it be strong enough? My three-year-old son has allayed my fears by using one of these tables as his playstation and a performance stage, to no adverse effect.

The board material is maple-veneered MDF, with edging strip ironed on to the exposed edges. The legs are solid timber, biscuit-jointed to the underside of the table, and the boards are also biscuit-jointed.

Finish the table with clear varnish or cellulose as the surface will need a good protection, especially on the edges.

—————————— Essential Tools ——————————

pencil, tape, square, marking knife, ruler, circular saw,
electric planer, biscuit jointer and 38 size 20 biscuits,
12 mm bevel-edge chisel, jack plane, block plane,
cabinet scraper, domestic iron, Workmate or
workbench, G-cramps

OTHER USEFUL TOOLS
table-mounted circular saw, palm sander

Coffee table

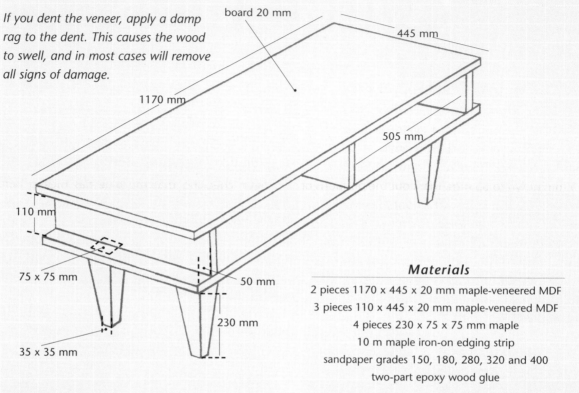

If you dent the veneer, apply a damp rag to the dent. This causes the wood to swell, and in most cases will remove all signs of damage.

board 20 mm

445 mm

1170 mm

505 mm

110 mm

75 x 75 mm

50 mm

230 mm

35 x 35 mm

You'll need to know

MARKING OUT
p. 18

PLANING
p. 20

BISCUIT JOINTERS
p. 23

Materials

2 pieces 1170 x 445 x 20 mm maple-veneered MDF

3 pieces 110 x 445 x 20 mm maple-veneered MDF

4 pieces 230 x 75 x 75 mm maple

10 m maple iron-on edging strip

sandpaper grades 150, 180, 280, 320 and 400

two-part epoxy wood glue

FIG 1

FIG 2

1 Mark out the boards, using a knife to cut through the veneer; make two cuts for each saw cut separated by the width of the kerf, to avoid splitting the veneer. Lay the uprights across the bottom shelf, clamped as shown in Fig 1. Cut the slots for the bottom shelf, and repeat the process for the top.

2 When preparing the maple for the legs, you need four lengths cut exactly to 230 mm. Mark the lengths with a knife and cut the barest distance from each knife cut, then use a sharp block plane to get the tops and bottoms perfectly flat and square (see Fig 2). As you plane, you will begin to see the knife cuts appear on the surface; don't plane below them.

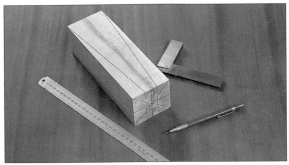

FIG 3

FIG 6

3 Mark each leg with a centre line marked on all four faces and both ends, as shown in Fig 3. The taper runs from the full width of 75 mm down to 35 mm. Mark out the positions of the legs, 50 mm in from the front and back edges and 70 mm in from the ends on the underside of the table base.

6 To apply the iron-on strip to the edges, set the iron to medium and apply firm pressure, checking that the glue has melted before moving on (see Fig 6). Use a block plane to remove the excess edging strip.

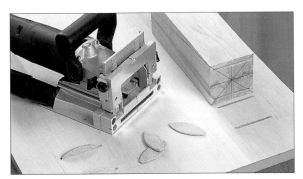

FIG 4

FIG 7

4 Clamp each leg up to the inner mark, ensuring that it is parallel to the edge of the base. Set the jointer plate to size 20 and cut the inner slot in both the leg and base (see Fig 4). Turn the leg around and repeat for the outer side. Repeat for each leg.

7 Use a palm sander to finish prior to assembly (see Fig 7). Glue the top first: place three bearers over the uprights top and bottom, then clamp the ends of the bearers. When gluing the legs, the weight of the table is sufficient to dispense with cramps.

5 Remove the legs and cut the waste, as shown in Fig 5. If you have a table saw with a 75 mm or better depth of cut, this is a straightforward operation; however, you may have to remove the waste by plane or even by two passes through a smaller saw. Bring the legs to a smooth finish with a plane, and then finally use a cabinet scraper. Use the offcuts to hold the legs in the vice.

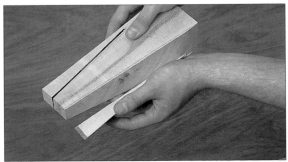

FIG 5

Computer workstation

This simple workstation, within the capabilities of even the newest weekend carpenter, is constructed from MDF held together with simple plastic corner joints; you could use plywood if you wish. The rigidity comes from the two shelves fitted at a low level, providing additional storage space for paper and files. An added luxury on this version is the retractable shelf for the mouse mat; it isn't essential, but it does free up desk space.

I designed the workstation to be placed in a corner of my daughter's house. She has the space, and the relevant corner is uninterrupted by doors or low-level windows. However, your requirements may well be different, so adjust the overall dimensions to suit. Another variable is the dimensions of your computer system. Most systems are fairly standard, consisting of a monitor, keyboard, the main housing, usually a tower, a printer and a scanner or fax. Measure your system before you begin to avoid problems, and if you're making this for a friend or a relative, check the dimensions of their system first.

No glue is used in the construction, allowing you to disassemble the finished workstation and transport it as a somewhat bulky flat pack.

Essential Tools
---

pencil, straightedge, tape, square, screwdriver, jigsaw, electric drill, 3 mm twist bit, block plane, Workmate or workbench, face mask

OTHER USEFUL TOOLS
table-mounted circular saw

Computer workstation

*The simple plastic corner joints that provide the support
for the MDF pieces are available in packs from DIY stores.*

**You'll need
to know**

BOARDS
p. 15

IRONMONGERY
p. 16

MARKING OUT
p. 18

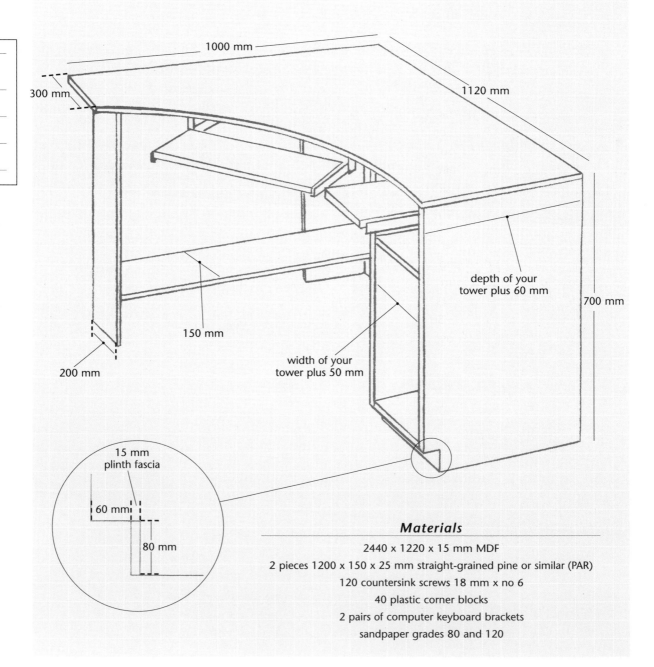

1000 mm

300 mm

1120 mm

depth of your
tower plus 60 mm

700 mm

150 mm

width of your
tower plus 50 mm

200 mm

15 mm
plinth fascia

60 mm

80 mm

Materials

2440 x 1220 x 15 mm MDF

2 pieces 1200 x 150 x 25 mm straight-grained pine or similar (PAR)

120 countersink screws 18 mm x no 6

40 plastic corner blocks

2 pairs of computer keyboard brackets

sandpaper grades 80 and 120

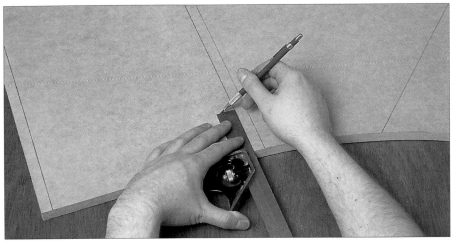

TIP

For the height of the upper shelf, I used an A4 folder plus 10 mm. Consider how you will use the shelf and adjust it accordingly.

FIG 1

1 Measure from the best corner of the sheet of MDF how far you want to come out in both directions and mark a line square to the edge, running forward from those points. Referring to the picture on page 104, the side that the fax machine sits on should be about 300 mm long, but the other side that will house the tower needs to be the full depth of your tower plus 60 mm to allow for plugs and any cabling. Ascertain the width of your tower, add 50 mm and two thicknesses of the MDF for the uprights. Mark another square line forward at this point. Square across to form a rectangle, which is the overall size of the tower housing. From the inner corner of this rectangle to the forward point of the 300 mm line is the springing point for the front curve. Draw this freehand with a soft pencil; don't make the curve too sharp, otherwise it may partially obstruct the keyboard. Move the sheet so that the top can be cut out with a jigsaw.

2 Ensure that the workpiece is well supported at both ends, and start the cut from the 300 mm line. A table-mounted circular saw makes the job easy. When you get to the inner corner of the tower housing, stop and cut from the other edge, using a straightedge as a guide. You can now mark out for the sides of the tower housing on the underside, as shown in Fig 1. Set your combination square to 60 mm, and mark the front and back for the positions of the corner blocks. Screw the corner blocks for the tower housing in place, ensuring that they sit exactly on the line, as shown in Fig 2.

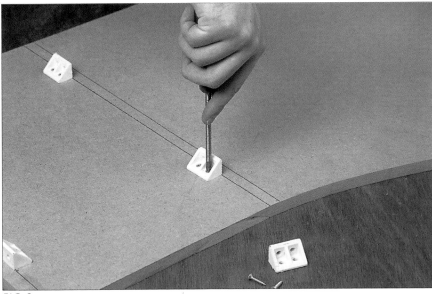

FIG 2

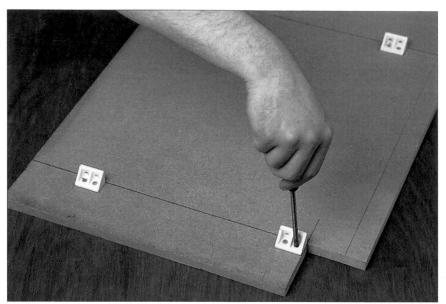

FIG 3

3 Mark out a left-hand and a right-hand side for your tower housing. The depth will be as pre-determined by the marking-out on the top, while the height will be 685 mm. On the bottom front corners, mark out a square 75 x 80 mm for the plinth fascia. Cut the sides out, plane off the saw cuts and lay the sides down on the workbench with the back edges butted up to each other. Mark across both inside faces together, the base with the underside sitting flush with the plinth cut out, and the shelf which sits just clear of the top of your tower. Use the combination square to position the connectors. Cut out two shelves, the widths determined by the marking-out on the top, and screw in place using four blocks per shelf (see Fig 3). For the plinth face, cut a strip 80 mm by the full width of the tower housing. Turn the housing upside down, and use a further two blocks to fix in place. Fix the unit to the top.

4 For the legs, cut three pieces of 685 x 200 mm and join two of them together using two blocks placed 60 mm in from the ends to provide the corner leg. A further centre block is used to provide additional support for the upper shelf; screw it in place when the shelf height has been determined (see Fig 4). Screw the corner leg to the top, coming forward about 50 mm from the edges to allow the passage of cabling behind. Place the end leg in from the back the same distance and about 75 mm from the end.

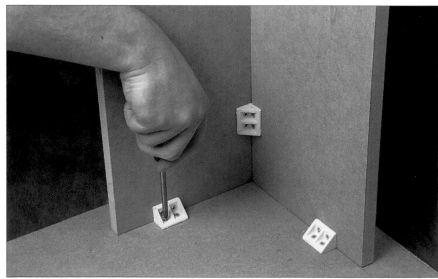

FIG 4

5 Cut the 150 x 25 mm pine to length for the shelves. The exact measurement is taken in situ, ensuring that the legs are square to the top. The upper shelf is fixed in place first. Mark the height (see Tip on page 107) on the inside face of the corner leg and on the inner face of the tower housing, fix two connector plates at each end and a further one at the same height to join the centre of the corner leg together. The underside height of the bottom shelf is the top of the lower corner block. Transfer this measurement to the single leg, fix the blocks in place and then fit the shelves, as shown in Fig 5.

FIG 5

> ## TIP
>
> If you are making this workstation for home use, you will probably not need to change the size of your computer housing frequently. If you are thinking of constructing it for office use, however, be aware that styles and sizes of housing change with alarming frequency.

6 Cut two pieces of MDF to the overall size of your keyboard and mouse mat, screw the sliders onto the edges, and fit the brackets that lower the sliders (see Fig 6). These generally have two positions; choose the upper for the keyboard and the lower for the mouse mat, giving clearance for the mouse when the slider is closed. Centre the keyboard on the curve and screw it into place. If you are using a mouse mat shelf, you will have to remove the top shelf of the tower housing to fix the mouse mat slider in place. Get help to turn the desk the right way up, and sand all edges prior to painting.

FIG 6

CD rack

My local joinery shop often sells me offcuts of prepared hardwood. If they have been commissioned to make a piece of furniture in an exotic timber, there will always be a small amount of waste left over. I rummage around and sometimes find the most extraordinary bargains, such as this piece of beautifully grained afrormosia. When you find a piece of timber such as this, a useful and elegant item to make from it is this modern CD rack.

You will need a router, although you could cut the slots by hand and remove the waste with a chisel. If you are new to using a router, this project will introduce you to using templates and a template guide bush fitted to the base of your router.

Like the Computer workstation project on page 104, this lends itself to a degree of personalizing: the number of CDs in your collection, the different thicknesses of those CDs – singles, doubles, etc., – and if you have a vast collection, you may want a wider rack, allowing you to store two or more rows of CDs side by side. Once it is finished, coat your rack with beeswax balsam or Danish oil, either of which will provide a beautiful lustre to the wood.

Essential Tools

pencil, straightedge, tape, square, screwdriver, electric drill, drill bits to suit the mirror plate holes, 25 mm gouge, 12 mm and 25 mm bevel-edge chisels, router with 6 mm and 12 mm straight cutters, block plane, cabinet scraper, Workmate or workbench

CD rack

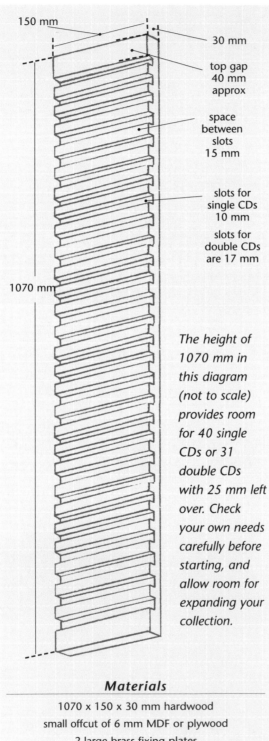

150 mm

30 mm

top gap
40 mm
approx

space
between
slots
15 mm

slots for
single CDs
10 mm

slots for
double CDs
are 17 mm

1070 mm

*The height of
1070 mm in
this diagram
(not to scale)
provides room
for 40 single
CDs or 31
double CDs
with 25 mm left
over. Check
your own needs
carefully before
starting, and
allow room for
expanding your
collection.*

Materials

1070 x 150 x 30 mm hardwood
small offcut of 6 mm MDF or plywood
2 large brass fixing plates
4 screws to fit fixing plates

You'll need to know

IRONMONGERY
p. 16

CABINET SCRAPERS
p. 20

ROUTERS
p. 22

FIG 1

1 Choose the face of the timber with the most attractive graining and smooth it with a cabinet scraper. Clamp the wood securely and draw the scraper towards you, slightly flexing across the width of the blade as you pull (see Fig 1). Some find it more comfortable to push the scraper away from them; it doesn't matter as long as you remove the surface and are left with a silky-smooth face.

FIG 2

2 Determined the number of 10 mm slots and the number of wider ones for double or boxed set CDs. Mark out across the face of the board, leaving a gap of 15 mm between each slot and a gap of about 40 mm at the top. Use a sharp craft knife or a marking knife held firmly against a square (see Fig 2). Choose a guide bush with a hole wide enough to allow the passage of the cutter you will be using. To cut the 10 mm slots I made two passes with a 6 mm cutter, and for the wider slots I used a 12 mm cutter with two passes. The bush outside diameter was 17 mm.

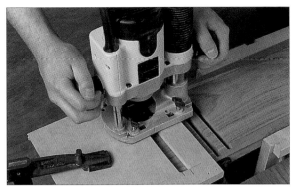

FIG 3

FIG 4

3 To mark and cut out your template requires a degree of precision and care. Measure the outer diameter of the guide and subtract the diameter of the cutter, then divide by 2 to give the offset from the bush to the groove you will cut. Add this measurement to the thickness of your slot, in this case 10 mm (see Fig 3). If you have a 10 mm cutter, you will only need to clamp a simple guide template the distance of the offset from one side of the cut line. If you have to do two passes, the offset needs to be added twice. Mark two parallel lines that distance apart, for instance 21 mm, as shown in the diagram below. The length of these lines should be 10 mm longer than the width of your timber at each end. Remove the waste from the template using your router fitted with a fence, taking great care that your cuts are true and do not go over the lines. When cutting with a router, follow the manufacturer's operating and safety instructions at all times, even for what might appear to be simple cuts.

4 Fit the guide bush to the base of your router. Clamp the work together firmly in your vice, clamp the MDF template in place centred over your knife marks, and make a practice pass with the bit lowered to just above the face of the work. Do not turn the router on for this pass, but look at the cutter carefully to ensure that it will not go past your marks. When you are sure everything is OK cut the slot, lowering the cutter a little more each pass to avoid any burning. Move the template along the workpiece to the next slot, ensuring that everything is stable and firmly clamped as you go (see Fig 4).

FIG 5

5 When all the slots have been cut, turn the timber over in the vice and place the fixing plates in position. These are ordinary brass fixing plates rebated into the rear surface. When positioning them, ensure that the fixing screws are not in line with a slot on the face, but are lined up with one of the gaps (see Fig 5). Using an 18 mm gouge will speed up this process.

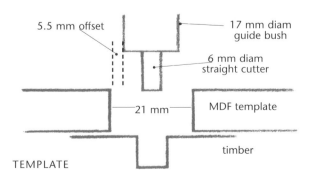

5.5 mm offset

17 mm diam guide bush

6 mm diam straight cutter

21 mm

MDF template

timber

TEMPLATE

Letter box

This project introduces cold-form bending, a technique that can, in relatively small projects, replace specialized steam bending; even better, unlike steam bending, it requires no expensive equipment. It also uses the fillet joint – a bead of viscous epoxy glue smeared across two adjacent surfaces, with the bead providing the actual joint. It is stronger than the timber it joins and has no loss of strength when used as a gap-filling compound up to 6 mm wide. Here, it is used to join the roof to the carcass.

To construct the roof, use layers of thin plywood or veneers built up to a thickness of 8 mm. I always use paper-backed veneers, which are cheap and don't tear or split along the grain. As only small amounts are needed for this project, see if local cabinet-makers or joinery shops have some offcuts.

The letter box here was fully veneered with maple, but you can stain or paint the carcass and use aero or skin plywood for the roof. This is a flexible plywood thinner than 2 mm that will bend to a radius of less than 100 mm.

The finish is two-pack polyurethane matt varnish, with the inside painted with bright red eggshell.

─────── Essential Tools ───────

pencil, tape, square, sliding bevel, Flexicurve or French curves, craft knife or scalpel, jigsaw, electric drill, 2 mm, 4 mm and 6 mm wood bits, belt sander, 12 mm and 25 mm bevel-edge chisels, jack plane, block plane, Workmate, G-cramps

Letter box

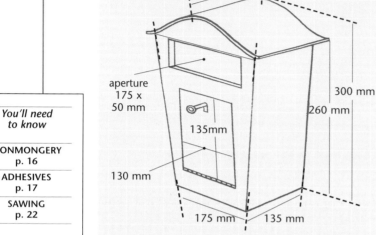

175 mm

aperture
175 x
50 mm

300 mm

260 mm

135mm

130 mm

175 mm · 135 mm

**You'll need
to know**

IRONMONGERY
p. 16

ADHESIVES
p. 17

SAWING
p. 22

Materials

650 x 435 x 9 mm exterior-grade plywood

650 x 435 mm sheet of paper-backed veneer (optional)

650 x 650 mm sheet of paper-backed veneer or
aero/skin plywood

1000 x 75 x 50 mm sawn pine or similar

130 mm brass or stainless steel piano hinge and screws

small brass cabinet lock and screws

sandpaper grades 100 to 240

PVA wood glue

two-part epoxy glue and colloidal silica

1 Cut three 330 mm lengths of 75 x 50 mm timber, plane or belt-sand the faces smooth, and select one block as a pattern. Mark the centre line and two square lines 300 mm apart, and use a Flexicurve or French curves to draw a slow curve with a slight upstand at the ends. The curve should lie roughly in the centre of the block. Cut to the line with a jigsaw. If the blade wanders during cutting, correct this with a belt sander. Use the pattern to replicate the marks on the other two blocks.

2 Glue each set of three formers together with PVA, then clamp and leave to dry. Cut the 9 mm ply to the sizes proscribed whilst the blocks are drying. Plane a bevel on the two short sides of the base, making the angle the same as the sides. Fit each half of the completed block in the vice and use a belt sander to obtain a good fit of the two parts. Ensure that the two surfaces not only fit but that they are as near as possible square to the edges.

FIG 1

3 Cut the skin plywood or veneer into eight sheets of 160 x 320 mm, four sheets running with the grain and four against. Place a sheet of newspaper over the concave section of the block and lay each sheet of veneer in place, alternating the grain direction. Lay a further sheet of newspaper over the final sheet, place the convex block in place and apply hand pressure. Check that each sheet of veneer is tightly compressed up against its neighbour and that you have an equal amount of overhang at each end. Unpack the stack and lay aside in reverse order. Mix the epoxy glue – with a 5:1 ratio you will need about 20 ml of resin and 4 ml of fast hardener. Wear gloves, work quickly and insert both sheets of newspaper (see Fig 1). Clamp and clean off any excess glue.

FIG 2

4 When dry – normally about two hours at 20 °C – unclamp and remove the newspaper and excess glue using a belt sander fitted with 120 grit or higher. You can accelerate the drying time by gently applying heat via a heat gun or a blow heater. Use a block plane to get the edges exactly flush, starting with the front edge, and then using a square to mark the two ends. Plane towards the centre to avoid splitting the ends (see Fig 2). Lay the edge of the roof section over the front and back walls and check the fit – 0.5 mm either way is acceptable. Sand or plane the roof line to achieve the fit.

5 Mark out the front panel to the given measurements, drill a hole in the waste parts and remove the waste with a jigsaw. Cut as close as you can with the blade and clean up with a chisel. (If you have a router, use it for this job and cut the corners of the openings square.) Test the replacement door panel for fit: you should have a gap of less than 0.5 mm all round, except for the bottom edge, which needs a gap of 4 mm to accommodate the hinge.

6 Cut the veneers, if you intend to use them. Each component will need to be cut with about a 10 mm overhang all round. If you are using paper-backed veneers for convenience, sharp scissors are the best method of cutting them. When you come to the apertures, use a sharp craft knife or a scalpel to exactly mark each corner with two right-angled cuts. Turn the veneer face up and join the marks using a steel rule, taking care not to cut past the pre-cut corners.

7 Apply glue to the veneers and clamp up; protect the veneer with paper, and don't clamp too tightly. When dry, clean up and cut the edges of the veneer flush as follows: front, back and door, all edges; sides, the top and bottom only; leave all the overhangs on the base.

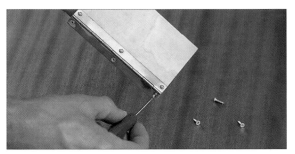

FIG 3

8 Cut the piano hinge to the same size as the bottom of the door and screw in place (see Fig 3). The centre of the knuckle should be exactly over the inner edge of the door. Screw to the front panel and plane the door if necessary.

FIG 4

9 Unscrew the door and remove the waste for the lock. Fit the lock and striking plate (see Fig 4), mark for the keyhole and cut with drills and chisel. Do not refit the door. To increase the viscosity of the glue mix and prevent it running down the joins, add up to 35% colloidal silica. When dry, shave off the overhanging veneers from the box with a block plane. Make another mix as before and glue the roof in place upside down. Pour in a generous amount of glue and use a rounded spatula to form the 6 mm fillet joint when the glue has started to cure. Replace the door and sand the box smooth.

Vanity unit

This design, influenced by the English Arts and Crafts and the French Art Nouveau movements, is a joint effort with my wife, Liza, who made the ceramic basin and mouldings. Although it is not a project for the beginner, providing your marking out is done with care, you should be able to produce a good-looking unit. Any reasonably stable hardwood can be used, although oak is the most stylistically correct for this type of design. The finish is a light coat of liming wax followed by a rich coat of beeswax.

When drawing out the shapes, take care that you do not make the curves too abrupt or too deep. Each curve should flow into the next. Achieving a balance for the upstand or splashback is very much a matter of trial and error. The return curves at the rear of the top have to balance with the outer edge of the upstand. The best method is to cut a template as shown on page 123; place this on the top and look hard at how the lines of the top and upstand intersect from every conceivable angle. The legs are splayed at 5 degrees from vertical – the front legs are splayed both out and forward, while the back legs only splay out.

--------- Essential Tools ---------

pencil, tape, square, marking knife, mortise gauge, screwdriver, crosscut saw, jigsaw, spokeshave, belt sander, electric drill, 5, 4 and 3 mm wood bits, countersink bit, router with 6, 12 and 25 mm straight cutters, plus a quarter-round cutter of 22 mm diameter with a 6 mm radius for the upper curve of the top and a 25 mm diameter ogee cutter with a 3 mm radius for the underside, biscuit jointer and 10 size 20 biscuits, range of bevel-edge chisels, jack plane, block plane, cabinet scraper, Workmate or workbench, sash cramps

OTHER USEFUL TOOLS
table-mounted circular saw, electric hand plane, bandsaw

Vanity unit

**You'll need
to know**

MARKING OUT
p. 18

PLANING
p. 20

SIMPLE JOINTS
p. 25

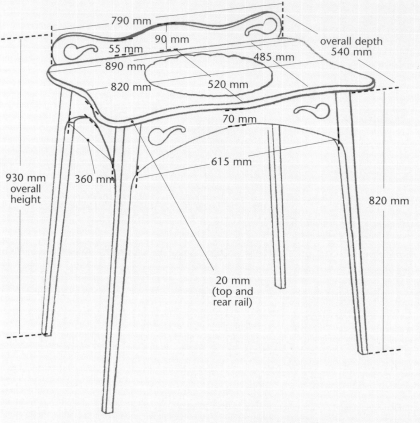

790 mm
90 mm
55 mm
890 mm
485 mm
820 mm
520 mm
overall depth
540 mm
70 mm
615 mm
930 mm
overall
height
360 mm
820 mm
20 mm
(top and
rear rail)

Do not use steel or brass-plated screws in oak, as they cause severe discoloration of the timber; instead, use solid brass screws. Always cut the screw hole with a steel screw of the same size first, withdraw the steel screw and replace with a brass one.

Materials

4 pieces 850 x 60 x 60 mm American white oak (legs)

850 x 170 x 35 mm American white oak (front rail)

2 pieces 420 x 170 x 35 mm American white oak (side rails)

700 x 100 x 20 mm American white oak (rear rail)

2700 (3 x 900) x 200 x 20 mm American white oak (top)

800 x 100 x 20 mm American white oak (upstand)

4 brass countersink screws 50 mm x no 10

18 brass roundhead screws 18 mm x no 6

6 stretcher plates

sandpaper grades 100 to 400

waterproof wood glue (Cascamite or similar)

1 Plane the legs true, 60 mm square and 850 mm long. When selecting the face and face-edge marks, bear in mind that the legs will splay out, so use the grain pattern to accentuate this if possible. If you use an electric plane, as shown in Fig 1, never plane closer than about 0.5 mm from the finished line, and keep your hand well away from the blades. Always finish with a jack plane, as this gives greater control and a far superior finish.

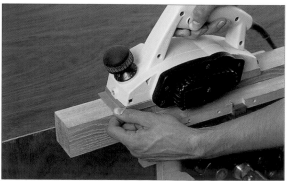

FIG 1

FIG 2

2 Select the legs according to grain type and direction for the best location, front or back pair, and mark accordingly. For the front pair, mark an 85-degree compound bevel with the lowest point being the front, outer corner (see Fig 2). For the rear legs, mark a simple bevel with the lower portion on the outer faces. For the front rail mortise, mark 12 mm with a mortise gauge 11.5 mm in from the front face. Cut all eight mortises using a router with a 12 mm straight cutter, except for the two inner faces of the back legs; these are cut to 6 mm wide and 7 mm in from the rear face. Set the depth of cut to maximum – using standard straight cutters this is 30 mm, and is just about sufficient.

FIG 3

3 Fig 3 shows the front left leg being marked for the curve between the upper end of the taper and the shoulder line of the front rail on the inner face. Repeat these markings on the front face and then for the other three legs. (The back legs should be marked on the inner and rear faces.)

4 The taper is marked out as in the diagram on page 141 – remember that the upper thickness, from whence the curve springs, is 40 mm. Make sure that the marks are on the proscribed faces, otherwise you will remove one set of marks when you cut the tapers.

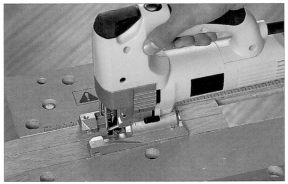

FIG 4

5 To remove the waste from the legs, use a jigsaw with the work mounted as shown in Fig 4. Move the leg along the Workmate as you proceed, to ensure you do not bind the saw blade. After the first cut rotate the leg through 90 degrees and use the non-parallel jaws of the Workmate to secure the job. Do not cut close to the line, especially when negotiating the curve – no matter how good the jigsaw, a small amount of wander on the blade is inevitable. If you have access to a bandsaw, use it for this step.

FIG 5

6 Any error in the cut of the inner faces of the legs can be removed with a spokeshave or a belt sander, using the 'nose' of the tool to finish the curve.

7 Mount the legs in a vice or Workmate, as shown in Fig 5, and plane the inside corner down to the 35 mm marks. This will leave a triangle reminiscent of a Gothic arch. Draw a line joining the two 35 mm marks across the face of the triangle and use a belt sander to remove the timber up to the line. The curved triangle that will result should be continued down the inner corner of the leg, feathering out about 100 mm below the shoulder lines. Mount each leg vertically in the vice and remove the end-grain waste down to the bevel marks, the bulk with the belt sander, finishing off with a block plane. Finish all faces of the legs with a cabinet scraper.

FIG 6

8 Cut the four rails to the sizes on page 120 – these are overlong, but will be cut to the correct length when the leg bevels have been marked. For the front rail, mark 615 mm along the upper edge, then lay the sliding bevel, set to 85 degrees, on the lower edge and mark with a knife. Slide the bevel along the length of the tenons – 30 mm unless you have cut the leg mortises deeper – and mark another line at each end. Square all lines around the rail, using the bevel and a square. Repeat for the smaller section rear rail. The side rails are 360 mm shoulder to shoulder, with the difference that the rear shoulder will be square to the upper edge; add the length of the tenons and cut to size. Clamp a batten parallel to the shoulder offset by the distance of the edge of your router to the edge of a 25 mm straight cutter, and remove the cheeks of the tenons (see Fig 6).

9 Cut away the excess portions – for the large tenons, 35 mm from the top and 20 mm from the bottom, for the smaller tenons on the rear rail, 25 mm from the top and 20 mm from the bottom. The measurements are taken from the shoulder line and are marked at 90 degrees to the shoulder, not the edge. Round off the edges of the tenons to fit the mortises, clean up the shoulders and assemble.

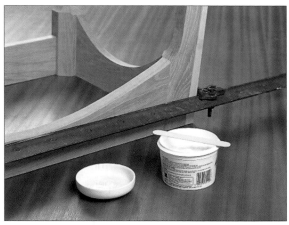

FIG 7

10 Once you have a good fit with all the shoulders meeting the legs, mark the top of the rails to replicate the bevels on the legs, disassemble and plane in the vice, checking the angle by using the sliding bevel. Before disassembling, make a small mark where the curve of each leg meets the adjacent rail. Once the top bevels have been planed, mark the centre of the front and side faces, measure down 70 mm for the front and 75 mm for the sides and mark. Use a long steel ruler to achieve a smooth curve between the three points. Draw the curve with a pencil, then remove the waste with a jigsaw. Reassemble and check that the flow of the leg curves into the rails and that the top bevel is flat all the way across the table. Cut six slow wedges from scrap and glue up, as shown in Fig 7. Don't place the cramp higher than shown, or you may shear the short grain on the curve of rail where it meets the leg. Tighten all cramps, check that the interior is square and clean up.

FIG 8

FIG 9

11 Cut the three parts for the top to 900 mm. Arrange them side by side, with the grain cupped alternately to minimise warping. Place any knots or defects in the centre, where you will cut out for the basin. Biscuit-joint the pieces, glue up and clamp together. When dry, place on the leg assembly with a 20 mm overhang to the rear and sketch out the edge profile, using a soft pencil. To achieve perfect symmetry, draw one half, trace it, flip the tracing paper and then press into the grain through the trace onto the other side with a hard pencil. Cut to the line with a jigsaw, smooth off with a belt sander, then rout the profile with a quarter-round cutter for the top edge and an ogee cutter for the bottom edge (see Fig 8), leaving a small return of about 3 mm at the base.

12 Sketch out the profile of the upstand on a 800 x 100 mm offcut of MDF or plywood. Use the front edge of the top as a template, reducing the length by 18 mm at each end. Place the template in position and adjust your lines as required. When you are satisfied with the shape, cut it out with a jigsaw and look at it in place again. If you're unsure that each side is symmetrical, use the best end, mark the centre and flip the template over.

TIP

Longer straight cutters, called pocket cutters, are available for cutting deeper mortises.
---

13 Transfer the template to the upstand (splashback), as shown in Fig 9, and cut out. Drill four countersunk holes from the underside of the top to fix in place, but do not fit yet.

FIG 10

14 Lay the top upside down with the leg assembly in place and fit the stretcher plates in place (see Fig 10). They will need to be bent slightly to accommodate the angled rails. Use only the slots that traverse the grain, as any expansion or contraction takes place across the width of timber, not the length. Place the screws in the centre of each slot. Turn upright, and screw and glue the upstand in place. Place the completed table on a flat, level surface, scribe around the base of each leg and cut to the line with a tenon saw. Then lay the ceramic basin upside down in place and draw round the rim, subtract the width of the rim and draw a second inner circle; cut to this second line and fit the basin with a bead of silicone mastic.

Tall storage chest

This project takes the weekend carpenter on to the next level, simple cabinet-making. To construct the drawers I used a professional, full-size dovetail jig; smaller jigs with a cutting width of up to 300 mm are also available. Look for rigidity in the plate, and ensure that the guide bush will fit your router. The jig should be mounted on a ply or MDF base, with a 25 mm hole drilled to a depth of 25 mm in one overhanging end to receive the protruding cutter when not being used for machining. The front of the drawer is placed face down on the top of the jig, with the relevant side mounted vertically in place. The off-set, which enables the pins and sockets of the dovetail to align, is achieved by using a small pin that screws into the side of the jig.

If you do not have access to a good-quality table saw and thicknesser, get the timbers prepared to size at a yard or joinery shop. I used ash, at the time of writing probably the cheapest hardwood. However, it tends to tear along the grain, so keep your tools perfectly honed, and expect to spend some time finishing with the cabinet scraper.

Essential Tools

pencil, steel rule or tape, square, marking knife, coping saw, drill with 3 mm and 4 mm twist bits, countersink bit, circular saw, router with 6 mm straight cutter and 45-degree bevel cutter, dovetail cutting jig and 11 mm dovetail cutter, biscuit jointer, 28 size 10 and 50 size 20 biscuits, range of bevel-edge chisels, jack plane, block plane, cabinet scraper, framing cramps, sash cramps or cramp heads, workbench

OTHER USEFUL TOOLS
table-mounted circular saw, electric hand plane

Tall storage chest

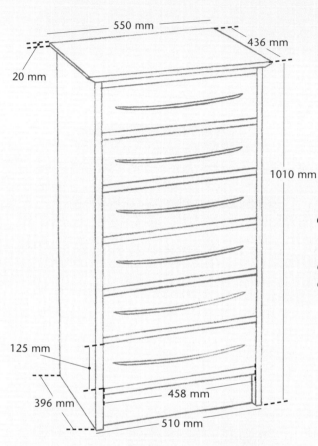

550 mm

436 mm

20 mm

1010 mm

125 mm

396 mm

458 mm

510 mm

Materials

14 pieces 385 x 43 x 20 mm hardwood, mitred at both ends (side runners)

14 pieces 470 x 43 x 20 mm hardwood, mitred at both ends (front and back runners)

2 pieces 990 x 396 x 20 mm hardwood (sides)

550 x 436 x 20 mm hardwood (top)

470 x 100 x 20 mm hardwood (false plinth)

6 pieces 458 x 125 x 20 mm hardwood (drawer fronts)

12 pieces 365 x 125 x 12 mm hardwood (drawer sides)

6 pieces 454 x 111 x 12 mm hardwood (drawer backs)

6 pieces 463 x 350 x 6 mm plywood (drawer bottoms)

505 x 970 x 6 mm plywood (chest back)

12 pieces 65 x 20 x 6 mm plywood offcuts (drawer stops)

35 countersink screws 50 mm x no 8

4 countersink screws 25 mm x no 8

6 chrome or brushed steel handles

15 mm moulding pins

PVA wood glue

sandpaper grades 120 to 400

FIG 1

1 Prepare the timber as per the cutting list; cut the top and sides to length and biscuit-joint them along the edges. Arrange all the mitre-cut runners on edge, with the shorter edge uppermost. Make a mark across the end grain 20 mm away from the short point at both ends, as shown

upper left in Fig 1: use one of the runners as a guide stick, hold it in place across all the mitres and then mark along the underside with a pencil. On the shorter side runners, mark and drill two 4 mm diameter countersunk holes, 50 mm in from the short point of the mitres, (see centre in Fig 1). Sort the runners into seven sets of four, two sides and a front and back, and cut a slot into the edge of the mitres for a size 10 biscuit, using the end-grain mark as a register mark for the jointer. Ensure that the work is securely clamped or that you screw the jointer to the workbench and use a fixed stop. The small amount of breakout on the short point, where the end of the biscuit will show, will not be seen and can be removed with a coping saw later.

2 Glue and clamp each frame, lay it flat with all glue wiped off, and ensure that it is perfectly square before leaving to dry.

FIG 2

3 When dry, release the frames and number them 1 to 7, on the back edge with each frame's best face up. Check that they are uniform, and if necessary plane the outer edges until they are all the same width and all square to the front edge. Stack the frames, ensuring that they are flat and level. Cut 12 offcuts of plywood into small trapezia, as shown in Fig 2; to form drawer stops. Glue and pin them in place to the six lower frames, with the front edge of the plywood back 20 mm from the front edge of the frame, i.e. the thickness of the drawer fronts.

FIG 3

4 Fig 3 shows two drawer fronts mounted face down in the dovetail jig, with the thinner sides clamped face in. Ensure that the parts are cut perfectly square and the side is flush to the upper face of the front. When you place the fronts in position, check that what will be the top edge of the drawer will have a pin and not a socket. Adjust this by moving the work to the left or right.

5 Mount the guide bush that comes with the template on the underside of your router, push the plunger down and lock off. Insert the dovetail bit and adjust the depth to 11 mm. Be careful not to inadvertently release the plunge lock when setting the fine depth adjuster, or when you finish a pass – if you do, especially when the router is running, you will ruin both cutter and guide bush.

FIG 4

6 Insert the dovetail template in place, using the adjustment nuts to achieve an exact alignment of the cutting line on the template surface with the join between the front and side parts of the drawer, and start to machine. Always work from left to right, allowing the router to achieve full speed prior to entry, and make the cuts through both pieces of timber (see Fig 4).

FIG 5

7 Fig 5 shows clearly a fully machined joint still clamped in the jig and an exploded joint that demonstrates how the workpieces should look when you have finished the cut.

FIG 6

8 To cut a groove for the drawer bottoms, fit a 6 mm straight cutter to your router and set the depth of cut to 5 mm, with the distance on the fence 8 mm in from the bottom edge of the drawer sides and fronts (see Fig 6). These grooves or housings should stop short on both ends of the front by 5 mm. Square off the end of these housings with a 6 mm chisel. The sides can be routed the full length, as the housing will fall in line with the lowest socket, provided you have mounted the fronts correctly in the jig (see step 4).

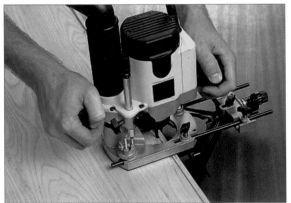

FIG 7

9 While the router is set up, rout out the carcass sides for the plywood back at this stage. As before, cut a 6 mm groove 5 mm deep, but this time adjust the fence to cut 5 mm in from the rear edge, as shown in Fig 7. Run the groove the entire length of both sides. Take care that the fence is parallel at the start and finish of each pass.

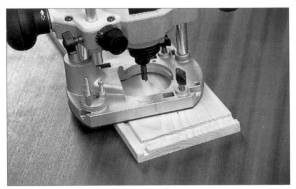

FIG 8

10 Cut a housing to the same depth, 12 mm wide, taken from 10 mm in from the end of the drawer sides and stopped at the 6 mm housing for the drawer bottom (see Fig 8). You can either use a 12 mm straight cutter or make two passes with the 6 mm one. Clamp a guide batten across the timber or use the router's fence across the end of the drawer side – the latter is far quicker, but take extreme care that the router doesn't 'rock in' when starting the cut. Cabinet-scrape and sand all the inner faces of the drawers.

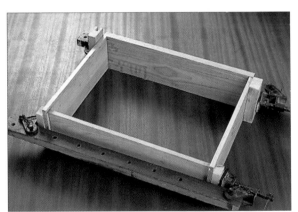

FIG 9

11 Glue up the drawers upside down, as shown in Fig 9. This allows you to check the positioning of the drawer back, and in addition will stop the back from sliding down the housing. Note that the glue blocks are pulled back from the drawer front to allow the dovetails to pull up tightly.

FIG 10

12 When fitting the bottoms to the drawers, you may need to use a block plane to achieve a slight bevel on the underside of the plywood. Glue each bottom in the grooves and pin the back edge to the underside of the drawer back (see Fig 10). Stack all the drawers interspersed with the frames on a level surface, check for any errors, especially on the width of the drawers, and rectify as required. No drawer should be narrower than the frames – if they are, you will once again have to plane the widths of the frames. Number the drawers on the back.

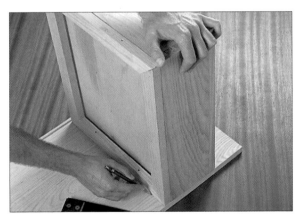

FIG 11

13 Lay one side down on the bench and, starting at the top, mark the position of each frame and drawer (see Fig 11), ensuring that they are square to the front edge of the side. Run a bead of glue where the frames lie, use a 3 mm drill bit to start the screws, and screw the six lower frames in place. Turn the assembly over and lay it on the other side of the carcass.

FIG 12

14 Repeat step 12 for the other side, checking continually that the carcass doesn't shift to a parallelogram (see Fig 12). When satisfied, leave to dry, lying on its back. Use a bevel cutter with a guide wheel to bevel the underside edge of the top. Cut to a depth of 14 mm on the front and both sides, leaving the back edge as is. Place the top on the carcass and centre it, which should leave a 20 mm overhang all round. Mark the position of the top frame from the inside of the carcass. Glue and screw the final frame to the top, making sure that the front overhang is correctly positioned. Replace the top on the carcass and screw and glue top in place via the frame sides.

FIG 13

15 Fit each drawer to its opening, planing the sides of the drawer where necessary and using a block plane to round the rear ends of each drawer side. Use a piece of thin card to achieve a consistent gap all the way around the drawer front (Fig 13). Fit the handles; insert and pin the back as for the drawer bottoms. Screw the false plinth using two blocks set back 40 mm from the front edge of the carcass.

Kitchen unit makeover

You can transform most kitchens with a little time, money and ingenuity. This 'makeover' retains the basic kitchen unit carcass, and replaces the doors, drawer fronts and workshop with your own custom-made versions. Most fitted kitchens are made from coated chipboard, which chips easily and becomes swollen and bloated when subject to moisture. Pay special attention to the sink cupboard: you may need to replace the whole thing, in which case buy from a cheaper range and discard the doors and false drawer fronts. If any part is swollen or the coating is damaged, replace it.

I recommend that all doors and drawer fronts be replaced with painted MDF or solid timber, and the work surfaces replaced with plywood covered in a waterproof material: tiles, slate, resin, or even real wood. I elected to use 300 mm square ceramic floor tiles, cemented to low-grade construction plywood using flexible tile cement.

The sinks are stainless steel inset bowls with a monoblock mixer tap serving both. If you need to move the sink, you will have to sort out the new feed for the taps and a waste pipe. Plan and complete any electrical work first. If you need additional sockets and have any doubt whatsoever about your competence, employ a qualified electrician.

To finish I used eggshell paint, after priming and undercoating the MDF. It's easiest to remove the doors for painting.

Essential Tools
---

pencil, straightedge, tape, square, screwdriver, mastic skeleton gun, panel saw, jigsaw, electric drill, 4 mm twist bit, 35 mm recessed hinge cutter, drill stand, jack plane, block plane, Workmate or workbench
For cutting ceramic tiles: tile cutter, angle grinder with stone-cutting disc, hacksaw frame with ceramic cutting file fitted

OTHER USEFUL TOOLS
table-mounted or hand-held circular saw

Kitchen unit makeover

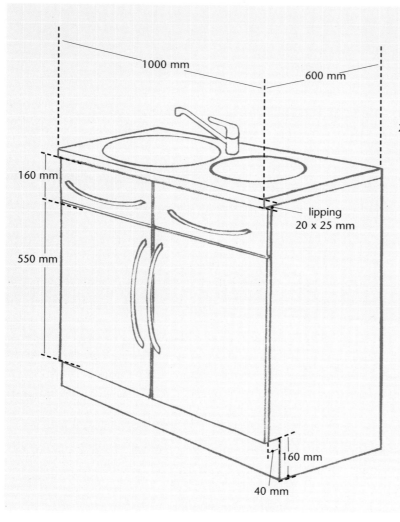

1000 mm

600 mm

160 mm

550 mm

lipping
20 x 25 mm

160 mm

40 mm

Materials

554 x 500 x 15 mm MDF per door
224 x 500 x 15 mm MDF per drawer
2440 x 1220 x 18 mm shuttering ply
2000 x 20 x 25 mm hardwood lipping
ceramic tiles and flexible tile cement
inset sink(s) and taps
drawer and door handles
silicone mastic
plastic corner blocks
30 18 mm x no 6 brass
countersink screws
sandpaper grades 80 and 100

The dimensions shown in this diagram are compatible with most self-assembly sink units available at DIY shops. You can adapt the measurements to fit existing or one-off units, but make sure that you keep everything in proportion.

You'll need to know

IRONMONGERY
p. 16

MARKING OUT
p. 18

SAWING
p. 22

WORKTOPS

FIG 1

1 Remove the existing worktop and sink, which will be fixed by angle brackets underneath. If you have pipes running through the work-top, these will have to be cut free. Repeat the shape of the old worktop in the shuttering plywood and fit in place, using new brackets if necessary. If you need to join the plywood, make the join meet over the place where two adjacent cupboards abut. Most manufacturers provide a paper template to cut the hole(s) for a new sink; drill a small hole to start the cut and then follow the line with a jigsaw, as shown in Fig 1.

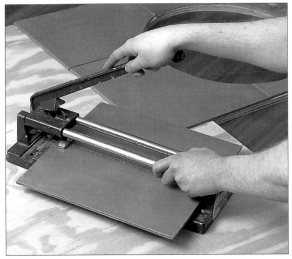

FIG 2

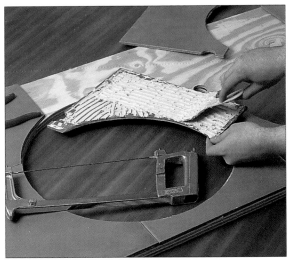

FIG 3

2 Loosely lay out the tiles on the worktop, allowing a 4 mm grout line between all joins; find a visual balance that keeps cutting to a minimum. Where possible, any cuts should be placed to the back or the sides of the worktop. It's a good idea to have a join running through where the tap hole will be. This will also give a neat line through the middle of the two sinks. Mark the tiles with a felt pen and cut them as shown in Fig 2. To cut curved tiles, transfer the sink cutout to the tile and then clamp the tile securely. Tape over the good part of the tile with masking tape to protect it should you slip, and run around the curved line with an angle grinder. If you haven't done this before, take it slowly. When you have ground down about halfway, the waste will break off and you will be left with a very sharp jagged edge. Use the grinder to smooth this off. When the tiles are cut, loose-lay them in position, check that the sink will fit and adjust if needed.

3 Spread the cement evenly on the back of each tile and twist into place. Some cement manufacturers recommend trowelling the surface to be fixed to; when dealing with large tiles it is cleaner, if a little slower, to trowel onto the back of the tile (see Fig 3). Use the cement applicator to ensure an even coating. Use tile spacers or matchsticks to keep an even grout line, and continually check the surface height, tapping down or adding cement as necessary.

FIG 4

4 When the tile cement is dry, usually the following day, cut and fit the edge beading. This should be the width of the tiles plus the ply and about 8–12 mm thick. Mitre all the corners and screw in place (see Fig 4). If you wish, you can counterbore and plug the screw holes. Grout the work surface and allow it to dry.

TIP

Wear gardening gloves while handling the sharp edges of tiles; this will minimise the risk of accidents.

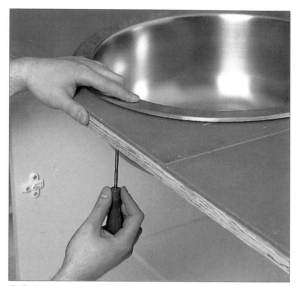

FIG 5

5 Place the sinks into the holes, seal with silicone mastic and tighten the sink clamps from underneath the worktop, according to the manufacturer's instructions (see Fig 5). As you tighten the screws, the mastic will be expelled from under the sink rim; wipe away any excess with a wet finger, using clean water from a bowl, not your saliva. Fit and connect the taps, using flexible hose connectors if you're a weekend plumber. The sink waste will need to be adapted if you are changing from one sink to a two-bowl system. A simple dimensioned sketch will be enough to solve your problem if you take it to a good plumber's merchant. Buy the push-fit waste system, not the glued type.

DRAWER FRONTS AND DOORS

FIG 6

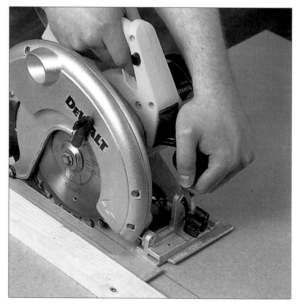

FIG 7

6 Remove each door and drawer from the existing units and lay it over a sheet of 15 mm MDF. Mark around each component, using the board to the most economical advantage (see Fig 6). Remember to allow for the thickness of your saw cut (the kerf) when marking. If any of your existing doors are damaged in any way, do not use them as a template, but substitute another of the same size.

7 Ensure that the board is firmly supported and fix a batten as a guide, then saw the components off, as shown in Fig 7 – using a circular saw makes the job easy. Stack them in groups of the same size, clamp in a vice and plane the edges smooth and square. You may wish to put a slight bevel on the face edges at this stage, using a block plane: I think about 4 mm all round looks attractive.

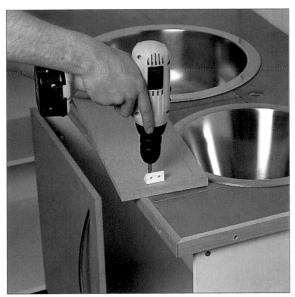

FIG 8

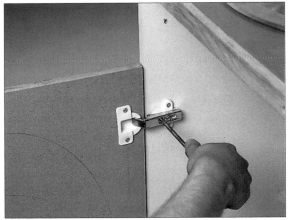

FIG 10

8 Fix a corner block at each end of the false drawer fronts (see Fig 8) and place in position on the cupboard. Inset the blocks by the thickness of the uprights, half the thickness in the centre of a double unit. Make sure that the drawer front is square and level, then screw in place. (Use a bradawl to start the screws off.) If replacing any practical (functional) drawers, simply unscrew the old front from inside the drawer and replace with your new version. With regard to fitting the doors, refer to step 10.

9 The handles I used come with a fixing template, and the only thing to be done is to choose their placing. Centre the drawer handles on the width of the drawer; a low placing looks better for the drawer handles. The door handles are placed 50 mm in from the edge and lifted towards the top, partly for ergonomic reasons and partly for a visual balance. Play around with the placing until you feel satisfied that the handles are in the best position in relation to each other. When you have decided, fix all handles in exactly the same position, ensuring that they are exactly square (see Fig 9). To cut the holes for the door hinges, see page 140, steps 7 and 8.

10 You will have to spend some time adjusting the fit of the doors; it is tedious but straightforward. There are usually two adjusting screws on each hinge: the larger allows you to move the hinge forward on the hinge backplate. By adjusting each of the pair of hinges using these screws, as shown in Fig 10, you can get the hinge edge of the door square to the edge of the cupboard. The smaller screw, often hidden inside the plastic casing, allows you to 'throw the door forward', adjusting the other edge. This is important if you have a pair of doors meeting, as the gap between them must be parallel and the tops at the same height.

FIG 9

Wall cupboard

This project, while using a different construction method to the kitchen unit makeover on page 130, is essentially a variation on a theme. The timber used for the doors, which are hung on an existing cupboard unit, is the highly fashionable maple, which is straight-grained and satisfying to work. Low-voltage lights are mounted inside the cupboards; if you wish to do this you will need to bring an electric feed up to the top of the cupboards. The transformer can be left just sitting above the cupboard, with the fittings mounted in the top.

I used glass-fronted doors for the cupboards. You can use glass doors fitted at low level for floor units, although I wouldn't recommend them if you have young children. Frosted glass blurs the cupboard's contents and is a compromise between to display or to conceal. If the contents are very much display items, use clear glass or, for a truly modernist look, Georgian wired safety glass.

In this project, it is assumed that you have mastered the skills required to true up your timber and that you are reasonably competent at making a mortise and tenon joint. The joint used in this door is a haunched mortise and tenon with 12 mm cut away, so that the rebate for the glass does not expose the tenon.

Essential Tools

pencil, straightedge, tape, square, marking gauge,
mortise gauge, marking knife, screwdriver, jack plane,
block plane, 6 mm, 12 mm and 25 mm bevel-edge
chisels, mallet, tenon saw, electric drill, drill stand,
35 mm recessed hinge cutter, router, 6 mm straight
cutter, 10 mm rebate cutter with guide wheel,
Workmate or workbench, sash cramps

OTHER USEFUL TOOLS
table-mounted circular saw

Wall cupboard

If you have good control of a mastic gun, it is possible to fix the glass in the cupboard doors by running a small bead of clear mastic around the inside of the glass.

You'll need to know

MARKING OUT
p. 18

ROUTERS
p. 22

SIMPLE JOINTS
p. 25

The diagram below gives the correct measurements for the haunched mortise and tenon joint.

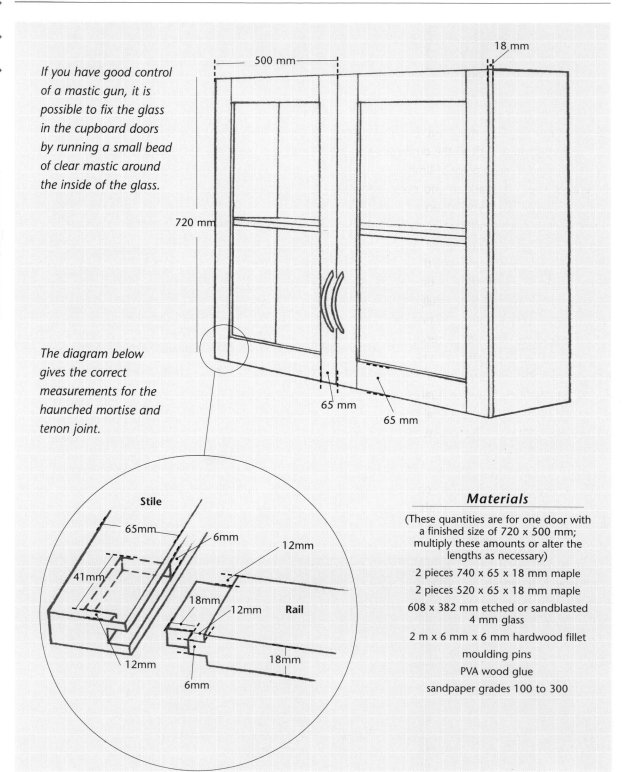

Materials

(These quantities are for one door with a finished size of 720 x 500 mm; multiply these amounts or alter the lengths as necessary)

2 pieces 740 x 65 x 18 mm maple

2 pieces 520 x 65 x 18 mm maple

608 x 382 mm etched or sandblasted 4 mm glass

2 m x 6 mm x 6 mm hardwood fillet

moulding pins

PVA wood glue

sandpaper grades 100 to 300

FIG 1

1 First, you need to mark out a rod, a simple measuring stick with all the dimensions to be transferred to each piece of timber. Starting at one end of the rod, mark an end point. Measure from this the height of your doors and mark them for the upright pieces, called stiles. In Fig 1 the line in the foreground on the rod is the end point; next, 12 mm along, is the line marking the haunch of the tenon, then the line of the cut back for the glass rebate, and then the line for the full width of the rail that will meet up to the stile. The horizontal timbers of a door are called rails and, because they are so much shorter, you can mark them between the stile marks. Normally all marks would start from the same end point, but to avoid visual confusion, they are placed in the middle. The final line in the foreground, just in front of the square, is the length of the tenon.

2 Line up all your stiles, cut them about 30 mm longer than the finished length and transfer the marks from the rod. Repeat this for the rails, but note that these will need to be cut exactly to length. Mark the mortises and tenons with a mortise gauge; when fully marked out at both ends, they should look as shown in Fig 2. The tenon marking is to the foreground, with the mortise marking out behind it. The rod is shown to the rear.

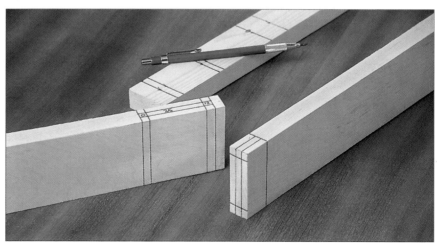

FIG 2

3 Use a router with a 6 mm bit to chop the mortises, remembering that the haunches are only cut to 12 mm deep (see Fig 3). Clean up the rounded ends of the mortise with a 6 mm chisel. If you have two fences for your router, one fixed to each side of the workpiece is a great help. Because the mortise in this project are cut with a router and the greatest safe depth of cut – 30 mm – is shorter than normal, the tenons will also need to be cut to this shorter length. It is, however, perfectly adequate for this size door.

FIG 3

4 Cut the cheeks and haunches with a tenon saw or a router; if you use the latter, use a guide and a block the same thickness as the workpiece to give additional support.

FIG 4

FIG 6

5 Dry-assemble, making sure that the frame is lying flat on the cramps, and check the frame for square (see Fig 4) – each measurement from corner to corner should be exactly the same. If not, adjust by moving one of the sash cramps slightly out of parallel, and retighten it.

7 The quickest method to mark the hinge positions is to use the old door you have already removed. Lay the doors edge to edge and transfer the marks, ensuring that the centre is the same distance from the edge as in the old door (see Fig 6).

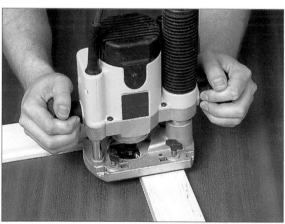

FIG 5

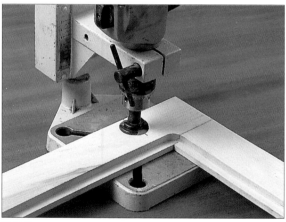

FIG 7

6 When dry, remove the frame from the cramps and lay it on the workbench. Secure and rout out the glazing rebate to a depth of 12 mm, using a rebate cutter with a guide wheel that will remove a 10 mm rebate (see Fig 5). If you are experienced at marking out, you may wish to do this step prior to following step 5. If not, doing it at this stage makes it much easier to work out what is happening. The cutter will leave radiused corners, which must be cut square with a chisel before you fit the glass.

8 Mount your drill in a drill stand and cut the holes for the hinges to the correct depth using a recessed hinge cutter (see Fig 7); in this case, the depth was 12 mm. You can use a router fitted with a 35 mm cutter to cut the hinge holes, but it is worth balancing up the cost of buying an expensive router cutter against that of a far cheaper drill cutter. Fit the glass using small maple fillets fixed in place with moulding pins. Hang the doors and adjust them by careful setting of the hinge adjusting screws.

CONSOLE TABLE LEG Page 54

CHILD'S BED HEADBOARD page 28

VANITY UNIT
LEG PROFILES
WITH MORTISE
POSITIONS
MARKED
page 118

60 mm

35 mm

7 mm

6 mm

55 mm

20 mm

60 mm

Rear left leg
inside face

60 mm

40 mm

600 mm

23 mm

35 mm

12 mm

105 mm

20 mm

60 mm

820 mm

Front left leg
inside face

VANITY UNIT SPLASHBACK PROFILE page 118

SUPPLIERS

United Kingdom

Tool manufacturers
De Walt Tools
210 Bath Rd
Slough, SL1 3YD
Tel: 01753 567 055

Black & Decker
210 Bath Rd
Slough, SL1 3YD
Tel: 01753 567 055

Stanley UK Ltd
The Stanley Works
Woodside
Sheffield
S3 9PD
Tel: 0114 276 8888

Tool retailers
Tilgear
Bridge House
69 Station Rd
Cuffley, Herts
EN6 4TG
Tel: 01707 873 434

S J Carter Tools Ltd
Gloucester House
10 Camberwell New Rd
London SE5 0TA
Tel: 020 7587 1222

Grinding wheels and jigs
C & M O'Donnell
Brough, Thurso
Caithness
Scotland
KW14 8YE
Tel: 01847 851 605
Email: odonnelltools@cs.com

Router tables & accessories
Trend Machinery & Cutting
Tools Ltd
Unit 6
Odhams Trading Estate
Watford, Herts
WD2 5TR
Tel: 01923 249 911
Email: mailserver@trend.co.uk

Ironmongery
Isaac Lord
Desborough Rd
High Wickham
Bucks
HP11 2QN
Tel: 01494 462 121

Two part epoxy glues & varnish
Structural Polymer Systems Ltd
Saint Cross Business Park
New Port
Isle of Wight, PO30 5WU
Tel: 01983 828 000
Email: info@spsystems.com

Wicker storage baskets
Chairworks
Unit 75-78 Chelsea Bridge
Business Centre
326-342 Queenstown Road
London SW8 4NE
Tel: 020 7498 7611

Hardwood retailers & timber yards
South London Hardwoods
390 Sydenham Road
Croydon, CR0 2EA
Tel: 020 8683 0292

North Heigham Sawmills Ltd
Paddock Street
Norwich, Norfolk
NR2 4TW
Tel: 01603 622 978

For further listings of retailers, the best place to get a national overview is from the many **woodworking magazines**:

Furniture & Cabinet Making
Guild of Master Craftsmen
166 High Street
Lewes, East Sussex
BN7 1XU
Tel: 01273 488 005

Traditional Woodworking
The Well House
High Street
Burton on Trent
Staffs, DE14 1JQ
Tel: 01283 742 970

Practical Woodworking
Nexus House
Azalea Drive
Swanley, Kent
BR8 8HU
Tel: 01858 435 344

The Woodworker
Nexus House
Azalea Drive
Swanley, Kent
BR8 8HU
Tel: 01858 435 344

Australia

DIY stores
Mitre 10
319 George Street
Sydney 2000
Tel: (02) 9262 1435
Freephone: 1800 803 304
(*outlets nationwide*)

BBC Hardware
Head Office, Building A
Crn. Cambridge &
 Chester Streets
Epping, NSW 2121
Tel: (02) 9876 0888
(*outlets nationwide*)

Two part epoxy glues and varnish
S P Systems Australia Ltd
4B Wilmette Place
Mona Vale
Sydney
NSW 2103

Timber suppliers
ABC Timbers and Building
Supplies Pty Ltd
46 Auburn Road
Regents Park 2143
Tel: (02) 9645 2511

Australian Treated Timber Sales
Brisbane 4000
Tel: 1 800 06 0685

Bowens Timber and Building
Supplies
135-173 Macaulay Road
North Melbourne 3051
Tel: (03) 9328 1041

New Zealand

DIY stores
Mitre 10 Support Centre
Head Office:
182 Wairau Rd
Glenfield
Auckland
Tel: 09 443 9900
(*outlets nationwide*)

Placemakers Support Office
150 Marua Rd
Private Bag 14942
Panmure
Auckland
Tel: 09 525 5100

South Africa

Timber suppliers
Federated Timbers
14 McKenzie Street Ind Sites
Bloemfontein 9301
Tel: (051) 447 3171
Fax: (051) 447 5053
(*outlets nationwide*)

Federated Timbers
39A Commercial Road
Arcadia, East London
Tel: (0431) 43 3733
Fax: (0431) 43 5240

PG Bison
4-5 Kwaford Road
Port Elizabeth 6001
Tel: (041) 453 1250
Fax: (041) 543 5046
(*outlets nationwide*)

DIY & hardware
Hardware Centre
14 Breë Street
Cape Town 8001
Tel: (021) 421 7358
Fax: (021) 419 6792

Hardware Centre
Union Main Centre
Old Main Road
Pinetown
Durban, 3610
Tel: (031) 702 2629
Fax: (031) 702 2581

Wardkiss Paint & Hardware
Centre
329 Sydney Road
Durban 4001
Tel: (031) 205 1551
Fax:(031) 205 2554

Tool retailers
J & J Sales
38 Argyle Street
East London 5201
Tel: (043) 743 3380
Fax: (043) 743 5432

Tooltrick
55A Bok Street
Pietersburg, 0699
Tel: (015) 295 5982
Fax: (015) 295 6151

Phillip Gardner can be
contacted at:
mail@philgardner.co.uk

CONVERSION CHART

To convert the metric measurements given in this book to imperial measurements, simply multiply the figure given in the text by the relevant number shown in the table alongside. Bear in mind that conversions will not necessarily work out exactly, and you will need to round the figure up or down slightly. (Do not use a combination of metric and imperial measurements — for accuracy, keep to one system.)

To convert	Multiply by
millimetres to inches	0.0394
metres to feet	3.28
metres to yards	1.093
sq millimetres to sq inches	0.00155
sq metres to sq feet	10.76
sq metres to sq yards	1.195
cu metres to cu feet	35.31
cu metres to cu yards	1.308
grams to pounds	0.0022
kilograms to pounds	2.2046

INDEX

page numbers for photographs and illustrations are shown in italics

A

adhesives
    Cascamite 17; *17*
    gluing up 41, 46, 53, 78
    PVA 17; *17*
    two-part epoxy 17, 41; *17*
    two-part filler 17; *17*
Adirondack chairs and stools 35, 36
arris 20; *20*

B

bark 78
bathroom accessories project 49-53; *48, 50-3*
beading 91, 95; *95*
bed project 14, 29, 31-3; *28, 30-3*
belt sanders 12; *13*
bending, cold-form 115
bevel edge chisels 9; *10*
birch-faced ply 15; *15*
birdhouse project 62-3; *60, 62-3*
biscuit jointers 13, 23-4; *12, 24*

biscuits 52
bits
    countersink *10*
    drill 11; *10*
    flat 11; *10*
    HSS 11; *10*
    masonry drill *10*
    multispeed *10*
    sharpening 25
    wood 11; *10*
blades 11, 25; *11*
block planes 10, 20; *9, 20*
boards
    MDF 15; *15*
    plywood 15; *15*
bradawls 9; *10*
bunk bed bolts 31-3; *33*
burnishers 25

C

cabinet project 14, 91-5; *90, 92-5*
cabinet scrapers 21, 112; *21*
    flat 10; *9*
    sharpening 25; *25*
Cascamite 17
CD rack project 23, 111-13; *110, 112-13*
chair project 11, 35-6, 38-41; *34, 36, 38-41*
chairs, Adirondack *see* chair project

child's bed project 14, 29-33; *28, 30-3*
    bunk bed bolts 31-3; *33*
    head board template 141
chiselling 21-2; *21*
chisels
    bevel edge 9; *10*
    firmer 9; *10*
    mortise 9; *10*
    sharpening 24; *25*
chopping board project 82-4; *82-4*
circular saws 12, 22; *11*
coffee table project 102-3; *101, 102-3*
cold-form bending 115
computer workstation project 105-9; *104, 106-9*
console table project 55-9; *54, 56-9*
    template of leg 141
coping saws 9; *9*
corner blocks *16, 106*
corner cabinet project 14, 91-5; *90, 92-5*
corner halving 25-6, 91; *26*
countersink bits *10*
countersink screws 38
cramps 11
    G-cramps 11
    sash 11
crosscut saws 9; *9*
crossheaded screwdrivers *10*
cupboard project 18, 137-40; *26, 136, 138-40*
cutters
    12-13, 23; *12*
    hole *10*
    plug *10*
    pocket 123
    sharpening 25

D

detail sanders 12
diamond dressers 24; *24*
diamond stones 25; *25*
dividers 9; *8*
door furniture 16
dovetail jigs 125
dovetail saws 9
dowels 16; *16*
draughtsman's rules *8*
drawer fronts 131, 134-5; *134-5*
drawer runners *17*
drill bits 11; *10*
duckboard 11, 53; *50, 53*

E

egg and dart beading 91
electric drills 11
electric planes 20, 120; *11, 120*
epoxy resin 17, 41; *17*

F

face masks 13, 43
finger joints 87

firmer chisels 9; *10*
flat bits 11; *10*
flat cabinet scrapers 10; *9*
Flexicurve 116; *85*
footstool project 11, 35-8; *34, 36-8*
French curves 116; *85*

G

G-cramps 11
gauges
    marking 8; *8*
    mortise 8; *8*
glass doors 137
glues *see* adhesives
gooseneck cabinet scrapers 10; *9*
gouges 9, 61; *10*
grain 20; *20-1*
grinding wheels 13, 24
guide bushes *12, 23*

H

hacksaws 9; *9*
halving joints *26*
handles 135; *135*
hardwoods 14, 19, 49, 111; *14, 78*
haunched mortise and tenon joints 27, 137, 139; *25, 138-9*
health and safety kit *13*
hinges 16
    Blum hinges *17*
    brass 67
    piano 67
hiring tools 13
hole cutters 11; *10*
hollow-ground bevels 24
honing *25*
housing 27; *27*
housing joints *27*
HSS bits 11; *10*

IJ

ironmongery 16; *16*
jack planes 10, 20; *9*
jigs 24; *24*
jigsaw 11, 22, 53; *11, 22*
joints
    biscuit 13, 23-4; *12, 24*
    corner halving 25-6; *26*
    finger 87

K

kerf *62*
keyboard tray sliders *17*
kitchen accessories project 81-5; *80, 82-5*
kitchen shelves unit project 27, 43-7; *42, 44-7*
kitchen unit makeover project 15, 131-5; *130, 132-5*
knife rack project 84-5; *84-5*
knives 8, 19; *8*

L

letter box project 115-17; *114, 116-17*

M

magnetic catches 16; *16*
mail-order service 8, 16; *17*
marking gauges 8, 18-20; *8, 18*
marking knives 19
marking out 18-19, 24; *19-20*
masonry drill bits *10*
MDF 15; *15*; dust 13, 43
measuring rods *19*
mirror plates 16; *16*
mitre saws 9, 55; *9*
mitres, cutting 27
mortise chisels 9; *10*
mortise gauges 8, 18; *8, 18*
mortise and tenon
    haunched 27, 137; *25, 138*
    joints 26-7; *26*
mouldings *15*
mug holder project 51; *50-2*
multispeed bits *10*

O

orbital sanders 12; *13*

P

paring 21-2; *21*
picture rail shelf project 97-9; *96, 98-9*
plane irons 24; *24*
planes
    block 10, 20; *9, 20*
    electric 20; *11*
    jack 10, 20; *9*
    shoulder 10; *9*
    smoothing 10; *9*
planing 20-1; *20*
plug cutters 11; *10*
plywood
    15; *15, 88*
    cutting 88; *88*
    skin 115-16
power tools 11-13
    blades 12; *11*
    circular saws 12; *11*
    electric planes 12; *11*
    hiring 13
    jigsaw *11*
    safety 13
projects
    bathroom accessories 49-53; *48, 50-3*
    bed 14, 29, 31-3; *28, 30-3*
    birdhouse 62-3; *60, 62-3*
    cabinet 14, 91-5; *90, 92-5*

CD rack 23, 111-13; *110, 112-13*
chair 11, 35-6, 38-41; *34, 36, 38-41*
child's bed 14, 29-33; *28, 30-3*
coffee table 102-3; *101, 102-3*
computer workstation 105-9; *104, 106-9*
console table 55-9; *54, 56-9*
corner cabinet 14, 91-5; *90, 92-5*
cupboard 18, 137-40; *26, 136, 138-40*
kitchen accessories 81-5; *80, 82-5*
kitchen shelves unit 27, 43-7; *42, 44-7*
kitchen unit makeover 15, 131-5; *130, 132-5*
knife rack 84-5; *84-5*
letter box 115-17; *114, 116-17*
mug holder 51; *50-2*
picture rail shelf 97-9; *96, 98-9*
single wardrobe 65-9; *64, 66-9*
soap dish 52; *50, 52*
stacking storage units 87-9; *86, 88-9*
storage chest 125-9; *124, 126-9*
storage units 87-9; *86, 88-9*
table 55-9; *54, 56-9*
tall storage chest 125-9; *124, 126-9*
toilet roll holder 51; *50-1*
toothbrush holder 51; *51-2*
towel ring 51; *50-1*
vanity unit 9, 119-23; *118, 120-3*
wall cupboard 18, 137-40; *26, 136, 138-40*
Waney shelves 16, 77-9; *76, 78-9*
wardrobe 65-9; *64, 66-9*
workstation for computer 105-9; *104, 106-9*
PVA 17; *17*

R

rails 139
reclaimed materials 15; *92*
rods 18; *19*
router tables 13; *12*
routers 12-13; *12*
routing
    22-3; *23*
    cutters 23, 25
    direction of the feed 23; *23*
    guide bushes 23; *23*

S

safety at work, 13, *13;*
sanding machines 12
    belt sander 12; *13*
    detail sander 12
    orbital sander 12; *13*
sash cramps 11
sawing 22; *22*
saws
    circular 12, 22; *11*
    coping 9, 83; *9*
    crosscut 9; *9*
    dovetail 9
    hacksaw 9; *9*
    jigsaw 11, 22; *11*
    mitre saw 9; *9*
    tenon 9; *9*
scrapers
    cabinet 10, 21; *9, 21*
    flat cabinet 10; *9*
    gooseneck cabinet 10; *9*
screen project 71, 73-5; *70, 72-5*
screwdrivers, 9; *10*
screws 16, 38; *120*
scribing 79
set squares 9
sharpening stone 11
sharpening tools 24-5
    grinding wheel 13
shelves
    kitchen unit project 27, 43-7; *42, 44-7*
    picture rail shelf 97-9; *96, 98-9*
    project 16, 77-9; *76, 78-9*
shoulder planes 10; *9*
shuttering ply 15; *15*
single wardrobe project 65-9; *64, 66-9*
sinks 131-2, 134; *132, 134*
sliding bevels 8, 18; *8*
smoothing planes 10; *9*
soap dish project 52; *50, 52*
softwood 14, 19
spokeshave 10; *9*
squares 8; *8*
squaring 93
stacking storage units project 87-9; *86, 88-9*
Stanley knife 19
steam bending 115
steel rules 8; *8*
steel tapes 8
stiles 139
storage chest project 125-9; *124, 126-9*
storage units project 87-9; *86, 88-9*
stretcher plates *16*
stub mortise and tenon 27; *26*
Surform tool 57

T

table project 55-9; *54, 56-9*
    template of leg 141
table top *24*

tall storage chest project 125-9; *124, 126-9*
tenon, routing *23*
tenon cheek *21, 26*
tenon joints 27
tenon saws 9; *9*
tiling 133; *133*
timber
    birch-faced ply 15; *15*
    grain 20
    hardwood 14, 19; *14*
    plywood 15; *15*
    preparing 19-20
    shuttering ply 15; *15*
    softwood 14, 19
    veneers 14; *15*
toilet roll holder project 51; *50-1*
toolkit 8
tools
    buying 8
    hand 8-11
    hiring 13
    power 11-13
    scrapers *9*
toothbrush holder project 51; *51-2*
towel ring project 51; *50-1*

VW

vanity unit project 9, 119-23; *118, 120-3*
    splashback profile template 141
veneers, 14, 102, 115-17; *15, 102*
wall cupboard project 18, 137-40; *26, 136, 138-40*
Waney shelves project 16, 77-9; *76, 78-9*
wardrobe project 65-9; *64, 66-9*
wood bits 11; *10*
workbench 11
Workmate 11
workstation for computer project 105-9; *104, 106-9*
worktops 132-4; *132-4*

Y

Yankee screwdrivers *10*

420-063

144